# A CHRISTMAS VIGIL

*Study* by Ronnie McBrayer
*Commentary* by Judson Edwards

Free downloadable Teaching Guide for this study available at

NextSunday.com/teachingguides

NextSunday Resources
6316 Peake Road
Macon, Georgia 31210-3960
1-800-747-3016
©2019 by NextSunday Resources

# TABLE OF CONTENTS

## A Christmas Vigil

# HOW TO USE THIS STUDY

*NextSunday Resources* Adult Bible Studies are designed to help adults study Scripture seriously within the context of the larger Christian tradition and, through that process, find their faith renewed, challenged, and strengthened. We study the Scriptures because we believe they affect our current lives in important ways. Each study contains the following three components:

## Study Guide

Each study guide lesson is arranged in four movements:

*Reflecting* recalls a contemporary story, anecdote, example, or illustration to help us anticipate the session's relevance in our lives.

*Studying* is centered on giving the biblical material in-depth attention while often surrounding it with helpful insights from theology, ethics, church history, and other areas.

*Understanding* helps us find relevant connections between our lives and the biblical message.

*What About Me?* provides brief statements that help unite life issues with the meaning of the biblical text.

## Commentary

Each study guide lesson is accompanied by an additional, in-depth commentary on the biblical material. Written by a different author than the study guide, each commentary gives the opportunity for learners to approach the Scripture text from a separate but complementary viewpoint.

## Teaching Guide

In addition to the provided study guide and commentary, *NextSunday Resources* also provides a *free* downloadable teaching guide, available at NextSunday.com. Each teaching guide gives the teacher tools for focusing on the content of each study guide lesson through additional commentary and Bible background information. Through teacher helps and teaching options, each teaching guide also provides substance for variety and choice in the preparation of each lesson.

NextSunday
*Resources*

# STUDY INTRODUCTION

On December 17, 1927, the crew of the Navy submarine S-4 trolled beneath the waters of Cape Cod Bay, engaged in routine testing of their vessel. At the same time, the Coast Guard cutter *Paulding* traveled across the surface. Those traveling on the two craft never saw each other. The submarine broke the surface just in time to receive a death blow from the *Paulding*. The submarine, with its crew of forty, sank in less than five minutes. It came to rest more than one hundred feet below on the ocean floor.

Rescue attempts began at once. Due to inclement weather, it took twenty-four hours for the first diver to descend to the wreckage. As soon as the diver's feet hit the hull, he heard tapping. Survivors were trapped inside. Pounding out Morse code on the hull with a hammer, the diver discovered that six crewmen had survived the collision. With renewed efforts, the rescue crew struggled to reach these men before it was too late. Again, the weather would not cooperate. Every attempt failed. With their air supply dwindling, the six survivors tapped out in Morse code a final haunting question, "Is there any hope?"

This provocative question echoes across the craft we call Earth. By our own experience, we agree with the New Testament's words that all of creation groans for renewal and relief. The world hopes for something better. As part of this expectant world, we do the same. We hope for a better future for ourselves, our children, and our families.

Hope is the intangible fuel that moves the human spirit along when life appears untenable; when marriages fail; when sickness invades; when we face difficult decisions; or when we encounter inexplicable suffering in our lives and in our world. We need hope to live on this planet the same way we need oxygen in our lungs.

In our faith tradition, all hope is fastened to the child we find lying in a Christmas manger. Christians gather in houses of worship and around Advent wreaths to reflect upon the implications of his birth and to anticipate the day when hope will become certainty, when what we can only pray for now will become definite. Advent is a season to remember, but it is also a time to renew our lives of hope in the One born in Bethlehem.

# HEIRS ACCORDING TO THE PROMISE

*Galatians 3:23-29*

## Central Question

What difference does Jesus make in how I see and relate to God?

## Scripture

**Galatians 3:23-29** Now before faith came, we were imprisoned and guarded under the law until faith would be revealed. 24 Therefore the law was our disciplinarian until Christ came, so that we might be justified by faith. 25 But now that faith has come, we are no longer subject to a disciplinarian, 26 for in Christ Jesus you are all children of God through faith. 27 As many of you as were baptized into Christ have clothed yourselves with Christ. 28 There is no longer Jew or Greek, there is no longer slave or free, there is no longer male and female; for all of you are one in Christ Jesus. 29 And if you belong to Christ, then you are Abraham's offspring, heirs according to the promise.

## Reflecting

On May 14, 1804, the Corps of Discovery, led by captains Meriwether Lewis and William Clark, set out on one of the most ambitious and renowned expeditions in American history. President Thomas Jefferson, who had dreamed of such a journey for two decades, charged the captains and their thirty men with the task of exploring, mapping, and traversing a portion of the North American continent that no European American had ever seen. Lewis and Clark were also hopeful to discover the long elusive Northwest Passage, a greatly sought after waterway connecting the Atlantic and Pacific Oceans.

After more than a year into their eight-thousand-mile journey, however, the Corps of Discovery had exhausted their efforts at plying the Missouri River. The mighty watercourse that had carried them so far became only a trickle, easily straddled by any of the men of the expedition. No Northwest Passage existed. The Corps of Discovery would have to find new transportation to complete their journey.

With more than a little apprehension, Lewis and Clark were forced to leave their priceless boats behind, the very vessels that had carried them into the American West. Their trusted means of travel could no longer bear them across the most rugged and daunting terrain they had ever encountered. With horses acquired from local Native Americans, Lewis and Clark crossed the Continental Divide into a land simply marked "Unknown" on their maps.

The Law of Moses once carried God's people along on their spiritual journey. Like Lewis and Clark's trusted boats, it was more than sufficient for travel. But completing the journey—moving on to maturity—required another means of travel. For Christians, the coming of Jesus changes the way we complete our journey of faith. He has revolutionized the way we relate to God. Yet, to travel with him requires that we let go of what has brought us this far.

## Studying

Paul's letter to the Galatians is unique in that it is addressed to a group of churches rather than a single congregation. Paul visited the region of Galatia, in the central part of what is modern-day Turkey, on his first missionary journey (Acts 13–14). It is possible he visited the area again on a later journey, but such a trip is not recorded in the Scriptures. If Paul wrote this letter after his first visit to Galatia, then this book is one of the first New Testament books to be written. Regardless of the exact date, however, Galatians is one of Paul's earliest writings, and it addresses an

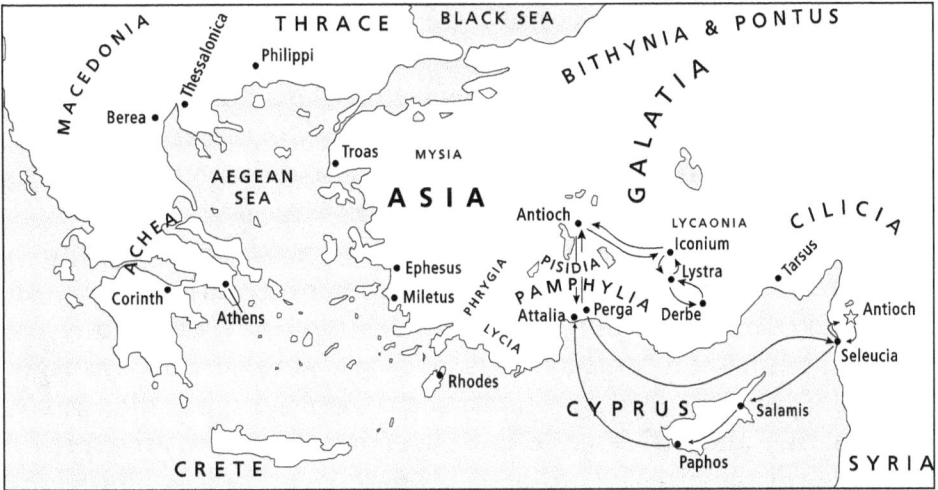

early Christian concern. This group of churches and individual Christians struggled with their newfound identity in Christ.

The first believers in Christ were Jews. As such, they had a commitment to the Mosaic Law that was nearly impossible to let go. As more and more Gentiles, or non-Jews, came to faith in Christ, a controversy developed over the role the law played in the Christian life. Paul's letter to the Galatians is a call to freedom from legalism, religious bondage, and stifled spirituality. Paul called the emerging Christian community to abandon their "boats" and launch into an unknown but wonderful journey of faith following Christ.

Capitalizing on Jewish history rather than ignoring it, Paul argues in Galatians that the bonds of slavery are forever broken and the captives set free in a way just as authentic as the Israelite exodus from Egypt. The redeeming and liberating God of the past, the God of Abraham, Isaac, and Jacob, has entered the world in the unique person of Jesus Christ to unshackle the imprisoned and enslaved, and to create the new humanity first promised to Abraham two thousand years earlier.

Paul's comparison to exodus, liberation, and renewal is clear in his use of the word "imprisoned" (v. 23). This was the condition of the ancient Jewish people and the reality of

> Don't misunderstand why I have come. I did not come to abolish the law of Moses or the writings of the prophets. No, I came to accomplish their purpose. (Mt 5:17)

humanity before the advent of Jesus. Still, the law, which preceded the coming of Christ, fulfilled its own purpose. It "guarded" (v. 23) humanity and served as a "disciplinarian" (vv. 23-24) until Christ came. The better translation of this word (Greek *paidagogos*), however, seems to be "custodian."

In Greek life, it was common for a well-educated, deeply trusted slave to watch over and care for the master's young children. The slave fulfilled the role of teacher, protector, nanny, and caregiver in a long-term relationship, lasting until the child reached adulthood. At that time, usually when the child was eighteen years old, the formal relationship dissolved. The child was now mature and no longer required a custodian. The grown child could legally receive the estate of his parents and enjoy all the benefits of being an adult.

Paul chooses this metaphor to explain the relationship between the Mosaic Law and the arrival of Christ. The law's purpose was to point the people of God toward maturity. It was not the *end*—as some early Jewish Christians wished it to be—but the *means* of preparation for Christ's coming into the world. The law could not serve as the "parent" of faith. This was not possible. The law could only play the role of caretaker, and now that Christ had come, that task was complete. To remain bound to rule keeping was to remain as children and to remain in bondage.

As the Law of Moses was once given to the nation of Israel as a way of teaching and directing them after their new emancipation from Egypt, Christ now provides that direction after his advent, cross, and resurrection.

The coming of Christ, then, fundamentally changed not only how God's people related to the Law, but also how God's people related to God. Jesus brought the family of God to maturity, "for in Christ Jesus you are all children of God through faith" (v. 26). The new humanity has arrived! Through faith, followers of Christ are no longer "underage" or under a custodian's oversight. They have

> Paul's words of equality in Galatians 3:28 were truly revolutionary. A common rabbinic prayer of the day was "Thank you God for not making me a heathen, a woman, or a slave" (b.Menahoth 43b-44a).

grown up to pursue Christ as spiritual adults and heirs, set free from immaturity and the law that accompanied it.

This is a maturity intended for the entire church. For "in Christ," all divisions of gender, age, ethnicity, socioeconomics, nationality, and authority are removed. All children of God enjoy the same status as co-inheritors of the grace and kingdom of God.

## Understanding

The Law of Moses could not give life or freedom. While it was instructive and useful, it could only constrict and confine. Still, these restrictions were not obstructions, but provided the context for the coming of Jesus and ultimately pointed to him. The advent of Jesus fulfilled the purpose of the Law and transformed its locked gates into an open doorway of freedom, grace, and love.

Thus, the book of Galatians challenges the reader to reassess the nature of his or her relationship with God. The relationship is not based on a set of laws, religious regulations, or rules, though these things likely influence one's spiritual journey. The relationship is grounded in knowing and following the person of Jesus. This is a radical departure for many, who have based their entire connection to God on rule keeping or "being good." But Paul is clear that such an approach to spirituality is nothing short of imprisonment.

> Because of Jesus Christ and because of what he is and did and does, my whole relationship with God is changed. I know that God is [now] my father and friend. I can enter into his presence with confidence and with boldness. He is no longer my enemy; he is no longer even my judge. I am more at home with him than with any human being in the world. And this is all because of Jesus Christ, and it could not possibly have happened without him. (Green, 69–70).

Christianity is not a heavy obligation to static, inanimate rules engraved in stone, or a complex combination of law and grace. Rather, Christianity is the free enjoyment of a relationship with a living person who is the exact representation of God. The

God of the Law is now present in Christ and calls people of faith to a greater maturity as we relate to him.

This maturity has practical implications beyond the relationship with God. The advent of Jesus deeply changes human interactions and relationships as well. The customary divisions of race, gender, nationality, and power are broken down so that God's children will grow into maturity as one family. The Law of Moses that once separated, isolated, and defined is now superseded by the unifying grace of God; and the immaturity of rules and partition is replaced by a new humanity, made possible by Jesus Christ.

## What About Me?

• *The Law was never intended to be the final means of relating to God.* Rather, God gave the Law to direct us to Christ. Like a road sign pointing toward a destination, the Law of Moses points people of faith toward Jesus. Jesus is the mediator between God and humanity, creating a relationship between heaven and earth. Allegiance to mere commandments is not the goal of the journey of faith.

• *We inherit nothing from legalism but are made mature children of God through a relationship with Jesus Christ.* The Law cannot lead us to maturity or make us heirs of God's promises and kingdom. Although it can show us our moral and spiritual failures, the Law is powerless to change or convert us. This power, which brings God's ancient promises to fulfillment, belongs to Jesus alone.

• *To commit oneself to a spirituality based on rule keeping is to be unnecessarily imprisoned.* Christ came into the world to set us free: from sin, death, judgment, and even the Law. The obligation placed upon us is not to keep the commandments, but to pursue Christ.

• *Letting go of our allegiance to the Law is not easy.* Relationships are vibrant and dynamic. They are not always easily defined. The comfort of the Law is its narrowness: it is clearly black and white. It draws clear lines around what is right and what is wrong. But

God wants us to be in relationship with him and follow Christ into the unknown. This leaves room for ambiguity that can only be resolved by clinging closer to Jesus.

• *The advent of Jesus does more than change how we relate to God; it changes how we relate to others.* The maturity that comes from following Christ transforms how we look at others. We no longer see the color of skin, the divisions of nationality or race, or other social barriers. All who follow Christ are counted as our brothers or sisters in the great family of God.

## Resource

Michael Green, *The Empty Cross of Jesus* (Downers Grove IL: InterVarsity, 1984).

# HEIRS ACCORDING TO THE PROMISE
### *Galatians 3:23-29*

## Jesus' Church

When Grace Country Cowboy Church began in Fort Worth, Texas, they said, "a posse was formed." They are trying to reach out to cowboys and cowgirls who would not attend the average church. The church welcomes anyone who enjoys old-time country music. They promise to "boot scoot for Jesus and two-step on the devil."

In Mayfield, Kentucky, every Sunday morning boaters gather at Kentucky Lake. They worship on the floating pavilion next to the marina restaurant. The pastor must be tempted to preach on fishers of men every service.

In upscale Manhattan, New York, in the arts community of Chelsea, The Gallery Church is made up almost entirely of single adults. Picture the cast from *Friends* discussing Song of Solomon.

In Union Point, Georgia, a church of ATV and motocross riders meets early each Sunday. In Denver, Colorado, a church that meets on Sunday nights is named—I am not making this up—The Scum of the Earth. The church is filled with punks, skaters, and people with tattoos, body piercings, and purple hair.

These churches reach people most churches do not reach, and that is wonderful. But we wish it weren't necessary, because it is not the church for which Jesus came.

Jesus' church does not have separate congregations for cowboys, boaters, singles, bikers, and those with unnatural hair colors. Jesus was serious when he said God is our Father and we all belong to one family. God's family seldom meets in the same church. We have churches for the rich, churches for the poor, churches for liberals, churches for conservatives, churches for white people, churches for black people, churches with Starbucks in the lobby, churches where the coffee only comes in one flavor and it's called "black," churches that function like neighborhood associations, churches that act like historical societies, and churches that say everyone is welcome—and yet everyone looks the same.

## Peter and Paul Argue about the Church (Gal 2:1-16)

After following Jesus for three years, it is surprising that Simon Peter believed in segregated churches, but he did for a while. Peter assumed that there would be churches for Jewish believers like him and churches for Gentile believers who were not like him. His church would sing *Hava Nagilah*, light menorahs on the Communion table, and eat matzoh balls at Easter. The other church would do whatever they did. Peter did not believe they could all go to the same church.

But Paul did. Paul thought that was the point—that we are all in this together. In a move that makes them sound like Baptists, folks decided to have a big business meeting at First Church, Jerusalem. Paul did not want a fight. He knew most of the leaders did not care for the kind of churches he was starting.

It was supposed to be a private meeting, but they quickly realized spies were there to cause trouble (Gal 2:4). No one paid attention to them, but the two sides were obvious. Peter wanted to run the Jewish Christian Church and let Paul and the Gentile Christian Church go their own way. Paul insisted that the gospel he preached to the Gentiles had to be the same gospel Peter preached to the Jews. Peter, James, and John—the pillars of the church—said, "That's fine." They shook Paul's hand and said, "You go to the non-Jews. We are right behind you, staying here with our people" (2:9).

This worked until Paul got news that made his blood boil. He went looking for Peter and an apostolic smack down. After the big meeting, Peter had visited churches of non-Jews, going to worship with them and joining them in the fellowship hall for lunch. However, some of the most conservative Jews from Jerusalem told Peter they did not want Gentiles in their church, and they also did not like Peter running with that crowd. Peter started distancing himself from his non-Jewish friends. When other Jewish Christians saw what Peter did, they began treating Gentile Christians like second-class church members (2:12).

Paul let Peter have it: "You are friends with non-Jews when your big-shot friends are not around, but when they show up, you act like Gentiles aren't worth talking to. We can't have two different churches—one Jewish and one Gentile. We're all in this by the grace of God. It's not about who we are. It's about God's love for all of us."

## Paul's Attempt to End the Argument (Gal 3:23-29)

For Paul, the key to ending the argument was the contrast between humankind's spiritual condition "before faith came" and after the coming of Christ. This section of Galatians is a reply to those like Peter who linked the covenant promises with the law (Charles B. Cousar, *Reading Galatians, Philippians and 1 Thessalonians* [Macon GA: Smyth & Helwys, 2001] 63). Paul recognized that linking the law to the covenant lessened the grace of Christ.

The law served as a temporary guardian. Paul viewed the Mosaic Law as a *paidagogos*—a household slave the Greeks used to watch over their children (3:24). This "disciplinarian" (NRSV) taught basic skills, but when the children were ready for school, a real teacher was brought in. A modern equivalent might be a British nanny (Mark Olsen, *Galatians: In Defense of Love* [Macon GA: Smyth & Helwys, 1994] 59–60). Like a nanny, the slave performed a necessary but temporary task. Now, with the coming of Christ, the law's task was finished. The children were turned over to Jesus. The metaphor is more about the law's curtailing of freedom than its teaching role. The law built a wall between Jews and Gentiles. The coming of Christ breaks down the barriers.

Galatians 3:26-28 sounds like 1 Corinthians 12:13 and Colossians 3:11; the three texts use the word "all" in the same way and contain a similar set of contrasts. These passages likely represent versions of a liturgy used at baptismal celebrations. Paul uses words they have spoken in worship to offer a conclusion to the debate.

The imagery of the baptized "clothing yourselves" (3:27) may bring to mind the church's practice of disrobing before baptism and putting on a new garment afterward. The one baptized takes on a Christ-formed life. They are becoming like Christ.

In the society of Paul's day, people took for granted that the male was superior to the female, the Jew to the Greek, the free person to the slave. Yet Paul catches a vision of a kingdom without prejudice—"no Greek nor Jew, no slave nor free, no male and female in Christ Jesus" (3:28). In Christ, patriarchal hierarchies no longer exist. When sons and daughters come of age and pass from life under the law to life in Christ, they become full heirs of the promises of God.

Paul's viewpoint was and still is hard for some to take. The idea of Jews and Gentiles together was culturally shattering. Slaves were not accepted as the equals of people born free. Paul plants the seeds of abolition (Olson, 61–62). Most were shocked at Paul's insistence that the distinctions of status between men and women counted for nothing when compared with the common experience of faith in Christ.

Those baptized into Christ share with him in the benefits of being Abraham's offspring and heirs according to the promise (3:29). The church of Jesus cannot neglect the implications of any part of Paul's claim. We tend to dismiss the equality of all as a peripheral issue for the church. We must realize that this is about how the Spirit speaks. If full partnership in the church is denied to anyone, then we all miss God's grace. Any way in which any person is treated as second class is contrary to the gospel. Those who follow Jesus cannot discriminate. We easily miss the revolutionary word that we are equal in God's family.

## The Argument Continues

Years ago, I was a pastor in a small town. Our church stood on a block in the kind of town square that makes you wish every town had one. Many of our members worked in a furniture factory, making gorgeous furniture that they could not afford. My salary as pastor was $14,000 a year, but the parsonage was filled with beautiful furniture. About 1987, the middle adult Sunday school class decided they did not want to sit on folding chairs anymore.

They worked out a deal with one of the managers in the factory's chair department. The fourteen members of the class spent $40 each to buy material for chairs that would normally cost about $500. The manager offered to let them make the chairs on a Saturday when the factory was closed.

What a great idea! Jesus was a carpenter. How could he not love this? The craftsmanship on the chairs was amazing—fine wood, deep finishes, exquisite details like brass trim. Any one of these chairs would suit the Palace of Versailles.

When I found out they were making exactly fourteen chairs, I curiously asked, "Couldn't we make a few extra?"

"The class only has fourteen members," came the reply. "We're the ones who are paying for the chairs and doing the work."

I naively asked, "What about when visitors come?"

"We still have the folding chairs, and if a member isn't there they can use one of our chairs."

I foolishly asked, "Won't you feel funny sitting in these beautiful chairs while visitors sit in folding chairs?"

"That's not going to happen," they insisted.

They were right.

Before the new chairs arrived, the teacher put a lock on the door. We had never had a lock on any door. He explained that they wanted the chairs to stay in the room and did not want the kids to get in there on Wednesday nights.

Several years later, Carol and I went back for the church's anniversary. They still had fourteen beautiful chairs in the room, but most went unfilled on most Sundays. The majority of the class was gone. The teacher had gotten angry and gone to another church. The young adult class was getting bigger. The older adult class was doing well, but the middle adults did not have anybody new.

What could be less surprising? That is what happens when we decide that the church will always be who we are now. That is what happens when we keep the best chairs for ourselves. That is what happens when we want some people to stay out of our church.

If our churches are going to look like the church Paul describes for the Galatians, we need more poor people to show us

Christ in the least of these. We need more rich people with portfolios in need of a good cause. We need people who drive SUVs and people who do not drive anything. We need PhDs and graduates of the school of hard knocks. We need people who kneel when they pray and people who put their hands in the air. We need people of various ethnicities to teach what their lives are like. We need conservative Christians who hold tenaciously to the central truths of our faith. We need liberal Christians who force us to think in new ways. We need young people to give us a sense of liveliness. We need old people who will give us a sense of liveliness. We need folks who grew up in other denominations to expand our understanding of faith. We need folks who share our religious heritage who appreciate its many good gifts. We need people who have sinned mightily and people who seem to have only gold stars by their names. We need cowboys, boaters, singles, and bikers.

What would happen if we believed in Paul's vision for the church? What would happen if different kinds of people were part of the same church?

People who are different push us to be better. People who are hurting teach us to love. People who ask questions help us find our way to better answers.

If we let the Holy Spirit have its way, churches could be churches for all kinds of people. How wonderful would it be if the church looked like the kingdom of God?

# Notes

# Notes

# 2

# IN THE FULLNESS
# OF TIME

*Matthew 1:1-17; Galatians 4:1-7*

## Central Question

What does it mean to call God "Father"?

## Scripture

**Matthew 1:1-17**   An account of the genealogy of Jesus the Messiah, the son of David, the son of Abraham.  2  Abraham was the father of Isaac, and Isaac the father of Jacob, and Jacob the father of Judah and his brothers,  3  and Judah the father of Perez and Zerah by Tamar, and Perez the father of Hezron, and Hezron the father of Aram,  4  and Aram the father of Aminadab, and Aminadab the father of Nahshon, and Nahshon the father of Salmon,  5  and Salmon the father of Boaz by Rahab, and Boaz the father of Obed by Ruth, and Obed the father of Jesse,  6  and Jesse the father of King David. And David was the father of Solomon by the wife of Uriah,  7  and Solomon the father of Rehoboam, and Rehoboam the father of Abijah, and Abijah the father of Asaph,  8  and Asaph the father of Jehoshaphat, and Jehoshaphat the father of Joram, and Joram the father of Uzziah,  9  and Uzziah the father of Jotham, and Jotham the father of Ahaz, and Ahaz the father of Hezekiah,  10  and Hezekiah the father of Manasseh, and Manasseh the father of Amos, and Amos the father of Josiah,  11  and Josiah the father of Jechoniah and his brothers, at the time of the deportation to Babylon.  12  And after the deportation to Babylon: Jechoniah was the father of Salathiel, and Salathiel the father of Zerubbabel,  13  and Zerubbabel the father of Abiud, and Abiud the father of Eliakim, and Eliakim the father of Azor, 14 and Azor the father of Zadok, and Zadok the father of Achim, and Achim the father of Eliud, 15 and Eliud the father of Eleazar, and Eleazar the father of Matthan, and Matthan the father of Jacob, 16 and Jacob the father of Joseph the husband of Mary, of whom Jesus was born, who is called the Messiah. 17 So all the generations from Abraham to David are fourteen generations; and from David to the deportation to Babylon, fourteen generations; and from the deportation to Babylon to the Messiah, fourteen generations.

**Galatians 4:1-7** My point is this: heirs, as long as they are minors, are no better than slaves, though they are the owners of all the property; 2 but they remain under guardians and trustees until the date set by the father. 3 So with us; while we were minors, we were enslaved to the elemental spirits of the world. 4 But when the fullness of time had come, God sent his Son, born of a woman, born under the law, 5 in order to redeem those who were under the law, so that we might receive adoption as children. 6 And because you are children, God has sent the Spirit of his Son into our hearts, crying, "Abba! Father!" 7 So you are no longer a slave but a child, and if a child then also an heir, through God.

## Reflecting

A father and his teenage son were embroiled in conflict. They wanted to make amends, so the son proposed a brilliant idea. For one month, the two would use "Fault Boxes." If the father somehow offended or hurt the son, rather than argue immediately, the son would jot it down on a piece of paper and put it in his box. His father would do the same with a box of his own. At the end of a month, they would exchange boxes in an effort at constructive criticism.

The boy kept a good list. Every time he felt his father was too demanding, he wrote it down and put the slip of paper in the box. When his father complained about him breaking curfew, jumped to conclusions, or refused to listen to him, he recorded it. Meanwhile, the son left a mess everywhere he went, burned through his allowance in a day and a half, and lived as if his father were his personal butler and chef. Consequently, the father filled his box with what appeared to be a full ream of paper.

Finally, the two sat down to dinner and exchanged Fault Boxes. The father went first and read through his failures. They talked about it, and he promised to be more understanding toward his son. Then the son received his father's box, which was overflowing with paper slips. But for every fault and misstep the son had made, his father had written the same message. Every piece of paper read, "I love you."

Likewise, if God spoke aloud to you right now, he would say what he has already said through his Son: "I love you, and I want you to be my child."

## Studying

God intends to bring humanity to maturity through his Son, Jesus, and not through obeying every letter of the law, fulfilling religious obligations, or keeping certain rules. God longs to bring every person into his family to live under the safety of his roof. Paul chooses adoption as a metaphor for this spiritual transition. God appropriates his redemption of humanity by receiving all who will believe as his children.

> What he was, he laid aside; what he was not, he assumed. He takes upon himself the poverty of my flesh so that I may receive the riches of his divinity.
> —Gregory of Nazianzus

Adoption was not common in Jewish society, but it was very common in the Roman world. Paul, as a Roman citizen, was familiar with this practice. Adoption was a Roman legal custom whereby an individual was granted all the rights and privileges of a natural-born child. Several Roman emperors chose a successor through adopting a trusted subordinate. Adoption was also a means of ensuring that one's estate went to a worthy heir after one's death.

For Paul, adoption thus became a fitting metaphor for how the relationship between humanity and God is transformed. Driven by the Father's love and purpose, Jesus brings us into the family of God as beloved children. While there is only one

natural-born Son—Jesus—this Son empowers all who believe and accept him to become God's children.

The adoption metaphor is a New Testament picture I greatly enjoy. My wife and I have a biological son and two adopted sons. These three boys are different in skin color, national origin, personality, and racial background. Yet they are all children of the same parents, share the same name, and live as brothers under the same roof. They share the same legal and official rights as sons and heirs.

This is what God has done for us. God has chosen to bring the diversity of humanity under the canopy of his home, to name us all as his children. We are not slaves, but sons, daughters, and rightful heirs of God's promises and kingdom (v. 7). As such, we cry out in gratitude and love, "Abba! Father!" (v. 6), a tender and affectionate address that no other god or divinity would permit.

Paul says this was accomplished "in the fullness of time" (v. 4). Christ came to earth during the unique period of the *Pax Romana*, or the "Roman Peace." This period of relative calm during the first and second centuries AD was marked by a common Greek language, expansive highways, stable lines of communication, and an unprecedented world empire. Political stability allowed the message of Jesus to travel quickly and relatively safely throughout the entire Mediterranean world—unlike the situation missionaries experienced in most other periods of history.

Paul's "fullness of time" language was also Jewish. Paul expresses here the great prophetic hope of the nation of Israel. With measured, patient, merciful steps, God has finally fulfilled the process of world history—and Israel's history in particular—to accomplish

> In Aramaic *abba* is originally a word derived from baby-language, equivalent to "daddy," but even before the advent of the Christian era the word underwent extension of meaning. It came to replace the older form of address common to biblical Hebrew and Aramaic (abi, my father) as well as the Aramaic descriptive terms for "the father" and "my father." The word *abba* came to be used by adult sons and daughters. Thus, the word came to acquire the warm, familiar meaning of "dear father." Jeremias maintains that it was an everyday word, a homely, family-word, a secular word, the tender filial address to a father. (Reynolds, 2)

divine purposes. Matthew's Gospel addresses this theme as well.

The Gospel according to Matthew begins with a genealogy. Exploring family history has become a common pastime for many individuals and families in recent years. Numerous web sites, books, and magazines teach people how to find old records and arrange expansive research notes. For Jews of the first century, maintaining family records was much more than a hobby. It was a way of staying connected with their ancestors and preserving the purity of their race, heritage, and separation from the world. Genealogies proved one's lineage and pedigree as a true member of the nation of Israel. The special rights and responsibilities of priests and Levites were tied to their ability to document their genealogy.

Therefore, Matthew begins his Gospel by summarizing Jesus' family tree. Apparently writing to early Jewish Christians, his opening verses authenticate Jesus' rightful claim to be the Messiah. By highlighting family connections with such significant Old Testament figures as Abraham, David, Jacob, and Judah, Matthew links Jesus with the grand, storied past of the Jewish nation and proclaims him the legitimate Savior of its future. The advent of Jesus came at just the right time, progressing from a divine history orchestrated for that moment.

The "fullness of time" also meant the bringing in of outsiders, or Gentiles, as adopted children. Matthew includes several such "outsiders" in Jesus' family tree. This open, adoptive stance is bolstered by Matthew's constant use of "Father" language when referring to God. Matthew uses the word "Father" forty-two times as a reference or address to God. By contrast, Mark and Luke, the other Synoptic Gospels, use such language only twenty times combined.

When one believes Jesus is God's Son, as Matthew intended his readers to believe, then one can relate to God as Father as well. At just the right time, Jesus came to make us children of God, as he is.

> Four women are included in Jesus' genealogy: Tamar (Gen 38:1-30), Rahab (Josh 2:1-21), Ruth (Ruth 1:1-18; 4:13-22), and Bathsheba (2 Sam 11–12). Tamar and Rahab were Canaanites and Ruth was a Moabite. Only Bathsheba was of Israelite ancestry.

## Understanding

There comes a point in any game or competition when someone makes the decisive move. In chess, maybe the rook takes the queen. In football, the offense makes the pivotal first down in the closing minutes or seconds. These are turning points when, though the game continues, the final outcome is basically determined. The decisive move in God's universe came at the advent of Jesus. At that moment, the final outcome was determined. All of human history had gathered to that point when God finally and ultimately came to earth in flesh and blood to make us God's children.

> **?** How is the birth of Christ a "game-changer" in human history? What does this imply about how we celebrate Christmas?

Thus, God desires to be far more than Creator or a Higher Power in the lives of people. God longs to be Father to his children. While "Father" is not the only title given to God, it is a powerful picture of God's love, care, and protection. Speaking of God as our "Father" is not an attempt to reinforce a paternal, male-driven religion or somehow prove God's gender, as if we could define God sexually. Rather, when speaking of God as our Father, we affirm his unconditional, parental love for all of his children.

This love is more than sentimental emotion. God has done all that is necessary to bring people into the family as children. In Christ, God brought the world to himself so that all are graciously welcomed. Jesus came as the uniquely born Son of God to make humanity the adopted sons and daughters of one heavenly Father. Followers of Jesus are thus not bound to keeping the law or serving an aloof, angry, or distant deity. They are free to enjoy an open, loving relationship with a God who gave all heaven had to bring them into his family and presence.

## What About Me?

• *The Advent of Jesus was not a haphazard or chance event.* The arrival of Jesus, the Messiah and Savior, is rooted in the history of the Jewish nation and for the benefit of the entire world. God moved and worked through centuries and circumstances until the time was just right for Jesus' birth.

• *With the birth of Jesus, God has done far more than say, "I love you."* God has demonstrated his love toward us by giving himself. God's love is not romantic or sentimental. It is powerful, active, and able to accomplish his purposes. God is not content merely to speak about love. God *shows* love with the birth of Jesus.

• *The ability to accept and address God as "Father" is a move toward spiritual maturity.* To see God only as a distant Deity or a Being unconcerned and unbothered by our lives and circumstances is to miss out on the wonder of being loved by the heavenly Father. The one who invites us to call him "Abba" has replaced the ancient paradigm of rules, laws, and religion with a personal relationship with the divine.

• *We are brought into the family of God by adoption.* Jesus, the uniquely born Son of God, has come to make humanity the adopted sons and daughters of God. There is no need to remain outside or to feel unacceptable or unworthy in the family of God. The grace of God is poured out in such a way that all who come are welcome.

• *No one is unacceptable or too much of an outsider for the Father's love and adoption.* The genealogy of Jesus is peppered with those who were outsiders and largely unacceptable to the society in which they lived. Yet God enthusiastically used these individuals to bring the Messiah into the world.

## Resource

J. A. Reynolds, "Abba," *Mercer Dictionary of the Bible*, ed. Watson E. Mills et al. (Macon GA: Mercer University Press, 1990).

# IN THE FULLNESS OF TIME

*Matthew 1:1-17; Galatians 4:1-7*

## An Advent Responsive Reading on Waiting

Leader: I am waiting for the moment when I become the person I keep thinking I should be,

**People: and I am waiting to feel no need for the approval of others.**

Leader: I am waiting to truly want the needy to have what I grudgingly give,

**People: and I am waiting to love other children with the love I have for my own.**

Leader: I am waiting for the church of Jesus Christ to act like Jesus Christ,

**People: and I am waiting to be the person I imagine God thinks I should be.**

Leader: I am waiting to serve no longer as a slave, but like an heir,

**People: and I am waiting to feel no longer like an orphan, but like a child of God.**

Leader: The promise of that for which we wait comes with Christmas.

**People: The hope we need was born in the fullness of time. The acceptance we desire has been given by God.**

We understand waiting. We wait for the day when we will get everything in order and be completely happy. We want to believe that life is supposed to be easy. We avoid the obvious truth that life is hard. Unfortunately, our lives will not become uncomplicated, because life is complicated. We will never solve all of our problems or put an end to all of our difficulties. The uncomplicated truth is that most of us have more medical tests in our future than in our past, more tears to come than we have already shed. We should not wait for simple solutions.

While we hope for perfect lives, we will continue to endure one heartache after another. We will keep falling short. We will enjoy only a tiny percentage of the music and poetry of the universe. We will be intimidated by the giftedness of others, incapacitated by our lack of discipline, and mesmerized by our fear of failure. We will be too patient with our own hypocrisy and too indifferent to our neighbors' needs. The carefree days will never last long enough. We wait for lives that will not be exactly what we hope for.

C. S. Lewis's *The Chronicles of Narnia* begins in a land where it is always winter but never Christmas. In Narnia, there are moments of cheer as well as sorrow, but the people forever wait for a joy that never comes. We know what that feels like. By one count, we spend an average of thirty minutes a day, one week a year, one year of our lives waiting in line. Those numbers seem low. We spend most of our lives waiting. We wait for something beyond what we can do on our own. Are we waiting for a hope that has already come?

## Paul Declares that the Wait Is Over (Gal 4:1-7)

Paul believes people have been waiting for the incarnation of Christ. There is no break between the preceding section on the promise shared by all (3:23-29) and the freedom of being God's children (4:1-7). The Judaizers arguing for the primacy of the law are wrong. Paul compares those under the law to minors placed under the protection of others (4:1). As small children, heirs had little freedom. Like slaves, they were told what to do. Even if the father died, their children's inheritance was placed in a trust; it made no difference for the time being.

"Guardians and trustees" (4:2) refers to the successive people to whom a minor was responsible under Roman law, the former until the age of fourteen and the latter until twenty-five. "Until the date set by the father" is curious. Under Roman law, the fixing of the time limit was out of the father's hands, so perhaps Paul wrote of some other legal system his readers understood.

The father in this illustration makes the best possible arrangements for his son.

"Elemental spirits" (4:3) may refer to basic religious teachings, but it could also mean spiritual agencies or demonic powers that affect people's destinies (Donald Guthrie, *Galatians* [Grand Rapids: Eerdmans, 1973] 112–13). Before baptism into Christ, they were in bondage to such spirits.

"The fullness of time" (4:4) suggests the critical importance of the moment in which God sent Christ. It marked the end of the old era and the beginning of the new. The Jewish world was waiting for the coming Messiah. The Roman world had contributed a measure of peace and developed communications linking the empire. The Greek language was widely used. Paul is convinced that the coming of Christ was not by accident but by divine appointment. Like a father setting a timetable for a child, God sent Jesus at a particular moment.

The Son of God was "born of a woman." Paul argues that Jesus came into the same environment as those who found it impossible to be justified under the law (Guthrie, 114). Paul does not say anything about a virgin birth. He either had not heard the story we read in Matthew and Luke (none of the Gospels were written yet), or he knew the story and chose not to mention it.

The ultimate purpose of the incarnation is our adoption into God's family.

Paul shifts from an image of an heir receiving an inheritance to one of a slave being redeemed. He shifts again to a third picture, that of an orphan being adopted. Inheritance, redemption, and adoption described the experience that followed a commitment to Christ. Paul asserts that God sent God's child in order to gain other children. This leads to the remarkable change in status from slave to beloved child.

God is addressed in both Aramaic and Greek. *Abba* was the Aramaic word children used for their fathers. As far as we know, Jesus was the first to address God in such an intensely personal way (Mark Olsen, *Galatians: In Defense of Love* [Macon GA: Smyth & Helwys, 1994] 64–65). There must have been some reason for the retention of Aramaic in writings designed for Greek-speaking people. The most probable explanation of the double form is a special sacredness attached to the actual word Jesus used, which the early church kept with a translation for those unfamiliar with Aramaic (Guthrie, 115). Perhaps newly baptized converts offered a prayer that began with these words.

The language remains male-oriented despite the liberating vision of 3:26-29. In Paul's world, "Father" served as a model for God. We should remember that the first creation narrative (Genesis 1:27–2:4) states that God created "male and female" together in the image of God (Frank Stagg, *Galatians/Romans* [Atlanta: John Knox, 1980] 20). God is neither male nor female. Paul emphasizes that we cry out to God, not to the law. We cry out as a child to a parent.

Paul chides anyone who accepts bondage to the law in place of the freedom of being a child of God. Christians have acquired a new status. Being a slave and being the master's child are mutually exclusive, so the children of God cannot keep waiting for freedom.

## Matthew Declares that the Wait Is Over (Mt 1:1-17)

The Gospel of Matthew begins in a way most writers would not choose—with a genealogy. This family tree sounds like a monotonous chant: "This guy was the father of this guy, and this guy the father of this guy, and this guy the father of this guy." We should not feel guilty if we remain unmoved by this section of Matthew. For us, this is a dull beginning to an exciting story. This lengthy recital of Jesus' ancestors is not the gripping start we might expect.

Matthew starts his Gospel with a genealogy for good reasons. The community to whom Matthew writes has roots in Israel but is increasingly welcome to Gentiles. The young church is dealing with how to be separate from the synagogue and yet true to the long-awaited Messiah. Jesus' genealogy intrigued them. Reading the names from the Jewish Scriptures was like discovering an old family Bible in the attic and finding in it a record of our ancestors' births, marriages, and deaths (Thomas Long, *Matthew* [Louisville: Westminster/John Knox, 1997] 7). This literary pattern (also found in Ruth 4:18-22; 1 Chr 2) was not merely a list of names, but a catalog of stories and memories. Matthew's readers must have read the genealogy slowly, savoring this roll call of faith, this list of the keepers of the promise God made to Abraham. The Greek word used for genealogy (1:1) is *genesis*, another way in which Matthew stressed the connection between the Hebrew Scriptures and the Gospel of Jesus.

Matthew introduces Jesus as the hope for which Israel has waited. The first line reads, "An account of the genealogy of Jesus the Messiah, the son of David, the son of Abraham" (1:1). Matthew describes Jewish history moving toward Jesus.

The enumerating of Jesus' family tree includes two significant surprises. The list is divided into three equal sets of fourteen generations: Abraham to David, David to the exile, and the exile to Jesus (1:17). The problem is that each of these three periods covers too many years to span only fourteen generations (Long, 10–11). The list is therefore not complete; several generations are missing. Furthermore, Matthew's genealogy is not in agreement with the one in Luke 3:23-38. Matthew's point is that Jesus' appearance in history is not an accident, but part of God's providence.

A second surprise is the inclusion of five women. Jewish genealogies do not include mothers. Early readers were likely surprised by the mothers Matthew chose and the mothers he skipped. Matthew did not list Sarah, Rebekah, and Leah, but instead included mothers with questionable lifestyles, mothers who were not even Jews, and mothers who had hard lives. However, each shocking name represents an amazing turn in Israel's history.

Tamar (1:3) pretended to be a prostitute and seduced her father-in-law (Gen 38). Tamar's place on Matthew's list of mothers is no more surprising than Rahab's (1:5). Rahab did not have to pretend to be a prostitute: she had a business in the red-light district of Jericho (Josh 2). Ruth (1:5) was a foreigner (Ruth 1–4). Bathsheba (1:6) was a victim of David's lust (2 Sam 11–12). Mary (1:16) was a teenage mother. Each of these women kept the hope of Israel alive. The birth of Jesus was the culmination of a centuries-long plan to send the world a Savior.

Jesus is the one for whom Israel has waited. Matthew makes the same point Paul makes in Galatians 4:1-7: that God sent Jesus in the fullness of time.

## The End of Our Wait

What does it mean for us to believe that Christ has come "in the fullness of time" and that our wait is over? We will still go through hard times, but the one for whom we wait has come. Jesus' hopes have become our hopes. Christ's vision has become our vision. Jesus talked about his kingdom as a great banquet, a hidden treasure, a pearl of great price; a kingdom where the prodigal and his brother celebrate together; a kingdom for the poor in spirit, the hungry, the merciful, the pure in heart, and those who mourn; a kingdom for widows and orphans, the sick and the lonely, the "has beens" and "never weres."

We do not have to wait to live in Christ's kingdom. Jesus inaugurated a way of life where hatred, racism, and revenge are purged from our memories, a kingdom where violence is not strength and compassion is not weakness. It may seem far away, but we can live as part of a kingdom where every person is loved; where male and female, black and white, rich and poor, old and young are treated equally; where the fellowship of the church is as wide as the grace of God.

If we catch Jesus' vision of peace, laughter, and wonder, if we have the courage to dream Jesus' dream, then we will understand that Christ's coming has already set us free to work for God's justice and live with God's love. Jesus has come and overwhelmed despair with hope.

# Notes

# Notes

3

# HE NAMED HIM
# JESUS

*Matthew 1:18-25*

## Central Question

What hard decisions do I face in serving God faithfully?

## Scripture

**Matthew 1:18-25**  Now the birth of Jesus the Messiah took place
in this way. When his mother Mary had been engaged to Joseph,
but before they lived together, she was found to be with child
from the Holy Spirit.  19  Her husband Joseph, being a righteous
man and unwilling to expose her to public disgrace, planned to
dismiss her quietly.  20  But just when he had resolved to do this,
an angel of the Lord appeared to him in a dream and said,
"Joseph, son of David, do not be afraid to take Mary as your wife,
for the child conceived in her is from the Holy Spirit.  21  She will
bear a son, and you are to name him Jesus, for he will save his
people from their sins."  22  All this took place to fulfill what had
been spoken by the Lord through the prophet:  23  "Look, the
virgin shall conceive and bear a son, and they shall name him
Emmanuel," which means, "God is with us."  24  When Joseph
awoke from sleep, he did as the angel of the Lord commanded
him; he took her as his wife,  25  but had no marital relations with
her until she had borne a son; and he named him Jesus.

## Reflecting

A lone survivor of a shipwreck washed up on the shore of a small,
deserted island. Though thankful to be alive, he recognized his

dire situation and began praying for God's mercy and rescue. Every day he scanned the horizon for help, but none came. Exhausted, he eventually began to make a life on the island. He built a hut out of driftwood and palm branches to protect himself from the elements and to store his few meager possessions. But then one day, after scavenging for food, he arrived home to find his little hut had somehow caught fire. The smoke rolled up to the sky.

As if shipwreck and loneliness were not enough, now his only home and few belongings were gone. He was stunned with anger, hurt, and doubt.

"God, how could you do this to me?" he cried out toward heaven.

Early the next day, however, the man awakened to the sound of a ship approaching the island. It had come to rescue him. Tears of joy streamed down the man's face.

"How did you know I was here?" he asked his rescuers.

"We saw your smoke signal asking for help," they replied.

Rather than driving God away, doubt may in fact bring God to us. When we feel as if all the faith we can muster is burning to the ground, it might be the necessary signal that causes God to appear to us in a way we never dreamed possible.

Doubt and apprehension must have filled Joseph as he contemplated Mary's inexplicable pregnancy. Even so, God spoke in the midst of those doubts and empowered Joseph to follow a difficult but rewarding path.

## Studying

While Matthew gives no attention to worshiping shepherds, singing angels, or swaddling clothes, he subtly connects the reader to Joseph's struggle leading up to Jesus' birth. The Christmas story justifiably centers on the baby in the manger, but for Joseph, the real drama of Advent occurred in the days and months that preceded the first Christmas morning.

Jewish marriages in the first century were completed in three distinct stages: engagement, betrothal, and the actual marriage. The engagement could be an extended period lasting for years—

even more than a decade. Marriages were often prearranged by the parents, so engagements could begin while the prospective husband and wife were still children. Engagements were not binding. They were, however, the first step toward a legal "contract" of sorts for the couple.

The engagement period was followed by an official and legally binding betrothal period. The betrothal corresponds somewhat with the engagement period in most Western cultures, but it was a far more serious relationship with distinct characteristics. For example, the betrothal lasted for one year, and while the couple did not yet live together or have sexual relations, the two were considered bound together in marriage. A betrothal could only be broken through formal divorce proceedings.

Following the many years of engagement and betrothal, the actual marriage ceremony took place. The groom arrived to escort the bride from her father's house to his own, thus symbolizing the change in their marital status. Only after this ceremony did the couple consummate their relationship and begin living together. While most North Americans find these customs unfamiliar, people in tribal or Eastern cultures in many parts of the world still follow them.

Joseph and Marry were in the betrothal stage of their relationship when Mary came to Joseph with disturbing news. She was pregnant. The text says, "she was found to be with child" (v. 19): a scandalous understatement. This was, of course, an unexpected "discovery." It was unexpected for Mary because she had not had sexual intercourse with any man. It was unexpected for Joseph because he assumed that Mary had broken their pledge of betrothal through an act of unfaithfulness.

So Joseph, working with the only reasonable conclusion he could make—that Mary had committed adultery—began making plans to "dismiss her quietly" (v. 19). Remember: the betrothal stage of the relationship was a legal arrangement as binding as marriage. Thus, only a declaration of divorce could break it. Joseph did not want to subject Mary to a public trial or put her at risk of suffering the

> Why might Joseph have considered divorcing Mary? What negative consequences might have come from going through with the wedding?

law's severe penalty for adultery (see Exod 20:14; Deut 22:20-27). Instead, he tried to find a way to end it inconspicuously.

During this period of contemplation, an angel of the Lord visited Joseph to announce the identity of the child in Mary's womb. In a dream, Joseph was told to proceed as planned with his wedding to Mary, "for the child conceived in her is from the Holy Spirit" (v. 20).

Joseph quickly and willingly obeyed God's instructions. He married Mary almost immediately and embraced the path God had for him. But surely he made this decision with a great deal of internal conflict. In marrying Mary rather than divorcing her, Joseph took upon himself the stigma, shame, and scandal of Mary's perceived transgression for the remainder of his life. Village living in the first century meant living among extended family members and tightly knit communities. There were likely few secrets in such places, little privacy, and electrifying gossip. Further, Joseph committed himself to caring and providing for a child that was not his.

**What reasons do we give for avoiding doing God's will?**

In fact, this child had no human father. Matthew and Luke are the only Gospel writers who explicitly mention the virginal conception of Jesus. Matthew uses a quote from Isaiah 7:14 as a fulfillment of the angel's message to Joseph: "the virgin shall conceive and bear a son" (v. 23).

The Hebrew word for "virgin" ('almah) can also mean "young woman" or "maiden." It is questionable whether Isaiah perceived the coming Messiah's birth as being accomplished without a human father, but Matthew emphatically interprets Isaiah's words that way. Although the Hebrew word is subject to varying interpretations, Matthew quotes the Greek Septuagint version of Isaiah, in which the Greek word (parthenos) clearly designates one who has never had marital relations.

Matthew's emphasis, however, is not on Mary's virginity—as important as that is. The emphasis is rightly placed on the fact that Jesus' conception was the work of the Holy Spirit.

Matthew wants his readers to see the conception of Jesus as a work of God—as miraculous as the creation of the cosmos itself. The power that brought Jesus into the world is the same power that brought the world into existence.

While the details of this holy conception remain an inexplicable mystery, the result is well established: the birth of Jesus was a miraculous act of God with the gracious consequence of "Emmanuel": God is with us! God came to earth in the flesh as a baby named Jesus.

## Understanding

Until God spoke to Joseph through the angel, Joseph operated under the assumption that Mary had been unfaithful to their vows of betrothal. It required great resolve and faith to trust God's message that the child in Mary's womb was of the Holy Spirit and not the result of Mary's adultery, but God empowered Joseph's faith and moved him to faithful obedience.

This renewal of Joseph's faith does not mean his life was suddenly and magically insulated from trouble just because he believed. On the contrary, Joseph now had to bear the scandal of his decision for the rest of his life. It is unlikely, however, that Joseph's faith was somehow less than it should have been. Countless numbers of good and godly people have suffered, gone without, and seen the worst of difficulties, not because they possessed inferior faith—a faith not big or strong enough to get them out of trouble. Rather, they suffered because their faith was so great.

How is your life different because of the choices you have made to obey God faithfully?

Those who suffer are often "too good for this world...and earn a good reputation because of their faith" (Heb 11:38-39). Virtue and faith can lead to suffering not because God is against us, but because God is for us and because God is using us to accomplish divine purposes.

Instead of a faith that professes the ability to change our circumstances, we need to cultivate a faith that changes *us*.

## What About Me?

• *Everyone faces unexpected, difficult decisions in following God's will.* Such decisions are not unique to biblical characters. We cannot avoid these challenging situations. Facing them requires discernment, prayer, and a commitment in seeking God's plan for the future.

• *Faith is a choice, not an emotion.* We may not always feel confident as we set out to do what we sense to be God's will. We may struggle with doubts, fears, and second guesses. But the proof of our faith is not our internal emotion; it is our determination to follow through and complete what we begin.

• *Taking an easier path, even a morally correct path, may not always be the right decision.* Joseph could have legally and rightfully divorced Mary. While he might have interpreted this as God's way of solving his dilemma, it was not God's will for him. God calls us to exercise genuine faith by doing what is right, not convenient or merely allowable.

• *Faithful obedience is not easy and often brings difficulty.* It is a mistake to think that obedience to God's will or way for our life will lead to instant success or ease. Many times obedience leads directly to conflict, misunderstanding, and ridicule from those who witness our actions. These ill effects are undeserved but often an outcome of faithfulness to God.

• *Obeying God's will means participating in something more significant than what we can do on our own.* Joseph could have never conceived that he would play the role of the earthly father of Messiah. When we embrace with faith God's will for our lives, we begin a journey that will take us places beyond our ability to imagine.

## Resource

Ben Witherington III, *Matthew*, Smyth & Helwys Bible Commentary (Macon GA: Smyth & Helwys, 2005).

# HE NAMED HIM
# JESUS
*Matthew 1:18-25*

## Patron Saint Joseph

Saint Joseph is the patron saint of cabinetmakers; confectioners; engineers; immigrants; house hunters; travelers; pioneers; pregnant women; fathers; married people; Austria; Belgium; Bohemia; Canada; China; Korea; Viet Nam; Manchester, New Hampshire; San Jose, California; Sioux Falls, South Dakota; and Nashville, Tennessee. It is an impressive list, but Joseph's connection to Nashville, for instance, seems tenuous at best. Joseph should be the patron saint of visionaries, romantics, and dreamers.

In our day, after several months of pretending to be interested in china patterns and bridesmaids' dresses, Joseph would finally figure out that the role of the groom is to say, "Yes, dear." The rabbi and organist would be lined up, the flowers ordered, and the honeymoon suite reserved. Planning for the bachelor party would surreptitiously begin.

## Joseph's Dilemma (Mt 1:18-23)

This is how the first Gospel tells the story of Jesus' birth. Before Mary and Joseph have "lived together" (Matthew means what you think Matthew means), Joseph gets the knee-buckling news that his fiancée is going to have a child that is not his. What is he to think? Will everyone know it is not his? Will they know that Joseph knows? Who is the father, really? If your fiancée is pregnant and you know you're not the father, it is hard not to view her behavior as inexcusable.

Joseph's life is suddenly in shambles, his trust betrayed, his future undone, and his insides torn up. Joseph has knots in his stomach. Nothing tastes right. His hopes and dreams have been destroyed. He wants to ask Mary, "How did this happen?" but he does not really want to know how this happened. He does not want to hear his buddies at work laugh and say, "Joseph, you sly dog." He cannot figure out how to fix this.

Joseph is a carpenter. He is organized, with each tool in the right place. Carpenters are exact—"Measure twice, cut once." All lines must be straight. A carpenter's life is logical and practical. Joseph's well-ordered universe is falling apart, and he sees no possibility of getting it back together any time soon. Orderly, careful Joseph is stuck in a mess that is not his fault.

After several sleepless nights, Joseph decides to try to put this behind him. His decision is logical, but "dismiss her quietly" does not sound heroic. We might wish Joseph would be a swashbuckling hero and take Mary far away to a place where they can live happily ever after.

As Matthew puts it, Joseph is a "righteous man," committed to the Law of Moses. According to Deuteronomy 22:20-21, Mary should be stoned to death. Yet Joseph wants to show compassion as well as righteousness. He interprets the law in the gentlest way possible. The right thing to do is to get on with his life and let Mary get on with hers. They should go their separate ways as quickly and quietly as possible.

Joseph's decision to divorce Mary quietly is not a predictable or easy response. Secrets do not always stay secret. How exactly would this one work? It could mean trying to hide a tiny girl as she grew less tiny. Maybe he could send her to a home for unwed mothers.

Then the story gets even more interesting. When Joseph thinks he has figured the best way out of this predicament and finally falls asleep, he dreams. First, the angel says, "Don't be afraid"—the same thing the angel said to Mary. Both Matthew and Luke include this advice. These words are important because Joseph, like Mary, has good reasons to be afraid. Joseph is caught in a disaster that could turn into a tragedy.

The angel continues, "Joseph, don't hesitate to get married. The Spirit made Mary pregnant. She will give birth to a son, and when she does, you will name him Jesus."

Matthew seems more interested in the name of the baby than in the actual birth, which gets little attention in his Gospel. "Jesus" is the Greek form of the Hebrew name "Joshua," which means "God helps" or "God saves." The second name, "Emmanuel," which means "God with us," is from Isaiah. Matthew quotes Old Testament prophecy and announces its fulfillment in Jesus eleven times. Saying Jesus' birth "fulfills" Isaiah 7:14 does not mean the prophet thought of Jesus when he first spoke those words. Isaiah originally gave this prophecy to address a political crisis in his own time, but Matthew finds that Isaiah's words point to more than Isaiah's moment in history. Matthew's version differs slightly, though. He identifies the woman as "the virgin," while Isaiah calls her "the young woman." Matthew quotes the Septuagint (the Greek version of the Old Testament) in which Isaiah's Hebrew word for "young woman" is translated "virgin" (Thomas Long, *Matthew* [Louisville: Westminster/John Knox, 1997] 14–15).

Joseph wants to know what to do about this problem with Mary, and an angel promises a baby will save them. It is a strange response—even for an angel in a dream.

## Joseph's Choice (Mt 1:24-25)

Even without an ultrasound, Joseph knows the child is a boy, but he also wonders if his experience was just a crazy dream. When he wakes up, he surprisingly does exactly what the angel commanded. One who believes righteousness is a matter of following the rules suddenly accepts the word of an angel. Earlier, Mary sang about the baby on the way, but Joseph is too stunned to sing. He takes his place in the story without songs or speeches.

Joseph wishes the angel had offered more specific suggestions. What is he supposed to do now? How many months does he have to get ready for Jesus' birth? How many weeks does he have to prepare for Christmas?

According to Luke, Mary goes to visit her aunt, but Joseph stays and waits. He could spend the time being frustrated; after all, he does not even get to pick the name. He could worry about supporting a wife and child. He could complain to his single buddies that he does not know anything about babies and hear them commiserate, "We don't know anything either." He could shrug his shoulders when his pregnancy-weary wife returns from Elizabeth's, unsure how to handle her discomfort. Instead, though, Joseph spends his time letting God create a place in his heart for Jesus.

## A Saint in the Background

Joseph stays in the background in the Christmas story. Luke hardly mentions him. The church has focused far more on Mary than on Joseph. Matthew's Gospel gives Joseph the most attention, and yet even Matthew tells us precious little about who Joseph was or what he did, and not one thing Joseph said. In fact, Joseph does not say a single word in the entire Bible.

In nativity scenes, Mary and Jesus are center stage while Joseph stands in the shadows. He is often hard to distinguish from the shepherds. In the crèche on the coffee table, if Joseph's head gets knocked off, as often happens to ceramic Josephs, you can always promote a shepherd in his place. In paintings, Joseph looks worn with fatigue, his face lined with anxiety. He seems like he would be more comfortable at a funeral than a birth.

It is easy to imagine Joseph as cautious and careful. When Matthew describes Joseph as just and righteous, we may picture an earnest, meticulous craftsman whose carpentry is all the excitement he wants.

Isaiah can wax philosophical about God's signs, but for Joseph this situation has nothing to do with ancient prophecies. Rather than "Emmanuel, meaning God with us," Joseph probably focused on his fiancée getting pregnant without him. The long-expected Jesus is coming quickly. Joseph assumes responsibility for a girl and her baby with only a voice in a dream to go on.

## A Saintly Decision

Everything changes when God calls Joseph. He still gets confused and frustrated, but nothing is ever quite the same. He does what God tells him to do. He stumbles along with no certainty of the outcome. Joseph takes his place in God's story, wading through the confusion and the mess, being led by God who has promised to save him. Joseph, like the rest of us, needed to be saved, so God sent a baby.

Leaving Mary would have seemed easier. Dreams are usually left behind. Ignoring an angel's whisper is not difficult. Even if Joseph could convince himself to believe Mary, no one else would. Acting honorably is easy—dismiss the dream and simply walk away.

Against all odds, Joseph pushes aside the arguments and follows the dream. He will marry this pregnant teenager and be the adoptive father of her child. He will take a huge risk on the basis of nothing more substantive than a dream.

This curious, astounding roll of the dice is Noah building the ark when no rain is forecast; Peter, James, and John dropping their nets to follow Jesus; Frodo Baggins hanging the ring around his neck; and Neo taking the red pill from Morpheus. Joseph is not safe, careful, or cautious. When faced with the choice of doing what is reasonable or taking a big chance, Joseph embraces the unexpected.

Joseph knows he will have to learn to deal with his lingering doubts about Mary. He will have to learn to ignore the snickers. The embarrassment is his too now. When the baby is born and people count the months, they will not think of Joseph as quite so honorable. He knows that he will gaze into the face of a baby and be unable to see the reflection of his own. He chooses the agony of sitting in the father's chair without being the father.

Joseph is a wonderful visionary who desperately wants the dream to be true. When Joseph marries Mary, perhaps he secretly thinks, "Whether it is true or not, this is what I want to believe."

What kind of man marries a woman who is having someone else's child? What kind of person pays attention to a dream and listens to an angel?

## The Decision to Dream

God's angels speak this word to all of us—"Don't be afraid to believe, to walk a different path, to follow dreams." We are tempted to a careful life: keep six of the ten commandments, go to church three out of four Sundays, give money we do not need and time we can spare, try to do more good than bad, offer some grace and some judgment, and believe the parts of the Bible with which we already agree.

God invites us to more: to wish for what is true. God's people long for God, even if they sometimes wonder what that means. The yearning for God itself is part of following God's dreams for us. Whenever we are dissatisfied with a cautious faith, it is because God wants more for us. God forever offers obscure intuitions that the truth is more wonderful than we have imagined, that there is a grace beyond anything we have suspected, a hope greater than we have dreamed.

God invites us to stop being cautious, embrace the unexpected, and allow the unexpected to embrace us. Dream of yourself loving God with all your heart—caring nothing about the expectations of those who have forgotten how to dream. Dream of the people you love letting go of jealousy and cynicism, offering only words of kindness to one another. Dream of a world where people take chances to help others and discover that God is not only our hope, but that God has placed that hope within us. Dream of God waiting for us to take one step in the direction of grace and discover the love that is always with us.

# Notes

# Notes

4

# WHERE IS
# THE CHILD?

*Matthew 2:1-12*

## Central Question

Am I a help or a hindrance to "strangers" who want to worship Jesus?

## Scripture

**Matthew 2:1-12** In the time of King Herod, after Jesus was born in Bethlehem of Judea, wise men from the East came to Jerusalem, 2 asking, "Where is the child who has been born king of the Jews? For we observed his star at its rising, and have come to pay him homage." 3 When King Herod heard this, he was frightened, and all Jerusalem with him; 4 and calling together all the chief priests and scribes of the people, he inquired of them where the Messiah was to be born. 5 They told him, "In Bethlehem of Judea; for so it has been written by the prophet: 6 'And you, Bethlehem, in the land of Judah, are by no means least among the rulers of Judah; for from you shall come a ruler who is to shepherd my people Israel.'" 7 Then Herod secretly called for the wise men and learned from them the exact time when the star had appeared. 8 Then he sent them to Bethlehem, saying, "Go and search diligently for the child; and when you have found him, bring me word so that I may also go and pay him homage." 9 When they had heard the king, they set out; and there, ahead of them, went the star that they had seen at its rising, until it stopped over the place where the child was. 10 When they saw that the star had stopped, they were overwhelmed with joy. 11 On entering the house, they saw the child with Mary his mother; and they knelt down and paid him homage. Then, opening their treasure chests, they offered him gifts of gold, frankincense, and myrrh. 12 And having been warned in a dream not to return to Herod, they left for their own country by another road.

## Reflecting

The chief information officer of a large company needed to speak to one of his employees about a problem with one of the computers at work. It was the weekend, however, so he dialed the employee's home number. A small child answered the phone in hushed tones: "Hello."

"Is your daddy at home?" the supervisor asked.

"Yes," the child whispered.

"May I speak to him?"

"No," came the response.

Surprised, but thinking his employee might be busy, the man asked, "Well, is your mother at home?

"Yes," again the child whispered.

"May I speak to her?"

"No," the child answered again.

Hoping to leave a message, the man asked, "Is anyone else there?"

The little boy said, "Yes, there is a policeman here."

This worried the boss on the other end of the phone, so carefully he asked, "May I speak to the policeman?"

The child answered, "No. He's busy right now, talking to my mommy and daddy and the fireman."

Growing even more concerned, the man heard what sounded like a helicopter in the background and voices shouting on the other end of the line.

"What is that noise?" he asked.

The little voice answered, "A hello-copter."

"A helicopter? What is going on there?"

"Well, the search team just landed in a hello-copter," the boy replied.

"Who are they searching for?" the man asked.

With a giggle, the little boy answered, "Me."

In this season of Advent, seekers search anew for Christ. He is near, but how helpful are we in directing others to him? Do we blaze a clear path for those who wish to worship Jesus with us—even those we normally consider outsiders?

## Studying

The arrival of the magi is one of the most celebrated elements of the Advent story. Traditionally, in Christmas plays and Nativity scenes, the "three wise men," as they are usually known, are found alongside the shepherds, singing angels, and barnyard animals in worship by the manger of Jesus. Historically and biblically, this traditional picture is inaccurate at best.

First, these were more than "wise men." A better translation is "magi." Magi were primitive astronomers by today's standards, but they were on the cutting edge of scientific and philosophical knowledge in their day.

Second, the magi were not "kings" from the "Orient" as the Christmas carol proclaims. There is no evidence that they were of royal descent, and they likely came from Arabia or Persia (modern-day Iran), not the Far East. When the carol "We Three Kings of Orient Are" was written, the "Orient" referred to what we would call the Middle East.

Third, there is no indication in the Gospel of Matthew of the number of magi. There could have been as few as two and up to almost any number.

According to Herodotus (c. 450 B.C.E.) magi (the plural of *magus*) were a priestly caste among the sixth-century Medes who specialized in interpreting the significance of human affairs through the observation of celestial phenomena (7.37) and the interpretation of dreams (1.107–108, 120, 128; 7.19). When the Persians conquered the Medes (ca. 550 B.C.E.), the magi apparently adopted the Zoroastrian religion of their conquerors, transforming it to the extent that they became its priests. Cicero (On *Divination* 1.91) indicates that no one was able to assume the throne of Persia without mastering the scientific discipline of the magi. In subsequent centuries the term came to be loosely applied all across the Mediterranean world to those adept in various forms of secret lore and magic. Thus by the first century C.E. it was applied to those of a particular class rather than to those of a particular culture or citizenship. (Gloer, 539)

Tradition says there were three magi (though some traditions mention twelve), and over time they were even given names: Gaspar, Melchior, and Balthasar.

What is known about the magi is that they came seeking "the child who has been born king of the Jews" (v. 2). The appearance of this king's star precipitated their journey and led them to Jerusalem. The magi interpreted this unusual star as a sign in the heavens; for them, it clearly communicated that something extraordinary had taken place in the world.

It was a common belief that signs in the heavens could be *fravashis*, angels or omens of a great man being born (Johnson, 257). Further, those in the Roman world expected the birth of a great leader (Barclay, 27). While it is impossible to determine what caused the magi to journey to Jerusalem, the goal of their expedition is clear: they came to worship Jesus, the Jewish Messiah.

The arrival of those who sought the one "born king of the Jews" troubled all of Jerusalem (v. 3), particularly the sitting king, Herod the Great. Herod came to power some forty years before these events. The Roman government had selected Herod as governor of Judea. He later received the title of "king." This was not an earned or rightfully inherited title, however. Herod was a political appointee. One "born" king of the Jews threatened his position. Herod feared the people might depose him in favor of one who rightfully belonged on the throne. It is obvious that Herod was troubled by this news. And when Herod was troubled, everyone around him was doubly troubled.

Herod the Great was infamous for his raging paranoia. The older he got, the more he feared losing his throne. He suspected conspiracy from everyone around him, and as a result he murdered those closest to him—including his mother-in-law, his wife, three of his sons, and a handful of other extended family members. The news of a legitimate threat to Herod's power was terrifying indeed.

Herod called the religious leaders of Jerusalem together, appeared most helpful to the magi, and inquired where the Messiah was to be born. Getting an answer, Herod sent the magi to Bethlehem to worship the newborn king under the pretense that he would follow them in worship once they found the child.

Bethlehem was and still is located on the outskirts of Jerusalem, about six miles southwest of the capital city. By the time of David, it likely numbered about five hundred people. By the time of Jesus, a thousand years later, the village likely still numbered less than a thousand.

Since it was a small town, and since they had the star to guide them (v. 9), the magi easily found Jesus. They entered the Holy Family's home (v. 11) and presented the first Christmas gifts ever given: gold, frankincense, and myrrh. In spite of distance, unfamiliarity, and Herod's hostility, they had finally arrived to worship the Christ.

## Understanding

Our communities, our churches, and our world are filled with people who desperately long to commune with God. They hunger and thirst for a spiritual relationship—for worship—and they journey through life trying to lay their hands and hearts on such a connection with the divine. But with no star to guide them, they don't always find what they are looking for.

Sometimes there are simply too many barriers: too many fences, too many dead ends, too much distance. Most of these obstacles are human-made. Seekers must overcome them in their search to find and worship the One who draws them.

Our churches and communities of faith must become places where seekers of God are welcomed, regardless of where their search began. Followers of Jesus can and should develop the skills of spiritual navigation. We can know more than the facts about Jesus and the Bible, and we can also know how to help people find Jesus. We can point people toward faith rather than pointing out our differences, and thus help those trying to connect with God to actually find God.

Religious institutions can become adept at welcoming those they want into the fold and alienating those who are unusual or unfamiliar. We sometimes build fences, string wire, and lock the gates to keep out everything we find fearful and threatening. In the end, we may succeed. But what will we have gained if we remain safe and comfortable while those who seek God on the outside wander about in confusion?

People of faith must find a way to open the gates and remove the barriers. We must smile at the world with hearts and faces of joy, not hiding behind locked doors, but standing with open arms and offered friendship. Better still, we should leave our religious compounds altogether and journey with these seekers who long to worship Jesus.

Tooling through the Deep South recently I saw an amazing sight. In a small town, tucked away between rolling hills and cotton fields, was a religious compound of sorts. The building and grounds were surrounded by a high chain link fence. The driveway was gated. Rolls of barbed wire were strung along the top of the fence. Large "No Trespassing" signs glared at passersby. It looked like a detention facility. Maybe it was. I don't know. Several very sad-looking children were sitting out front in the summer heat with long faces.

As the Encampment wilted away in my rearview mirror I couldn't help but think how it was such a sadly accurate representation of so much of Christendom. Fences. Walls. Gated doors. "No Trespassing" signs. Keep out. Let it not be missed that the accusation the religious community always brought against Jesus was this: "He is a friend to sinners." Could such an accusation be laid at the feet of the church today? Would such an indictment stick?

You don't have to travel to an obscure campground to see religious "Keep Out" signs. The establishment is very good at sorting the sheep from the goats and the wheat from the weeds. "This one is in. That one is out. This one passes. That one fails. This one is approved. That one is rejected." Through careful examination and religious inspection, only those with acceptable morals, beliefs, and lifestyles are allowed in the door. This is all done, of course, with God's blessing. For God is on our team. He is inside our fence. He authorized our "Keep Out" signs. (McBrayer, 128)

## What About Me?

• *Some people have traveled great distances to seek God.* The magi may have given years of their lives pursuing the Messiah. They traveled hundreds of miles. Many seekers of Jesus have been looking for him for a long time. These people are a great gift to the church. It is our responsibility to point them to Jesus.

• *Seekers of God can show up from unexpected places at unexpected times.* Not everyone who desires a relationship with God is found at the church at the scheduled time for Sunday worship. We're just as likely to find them in the marketplace, at a neighborhood barbecue, or at dinner with new friends. God's spirit speaks and moves where it will to bring people to faith.

• *Genuine worshipers of Jesus sometimes look and act differently than expected.* The wise men were of a different culture, language, race, and religious background than the Jews. Yet they came to worship the Jewish Messiah with more heartfelt desire than all of Jerusalem's leadership. They were outwardly dissimilar, but inwardly they sought the true God. External differences should not be a barrier. God looks at the heart.

• *The religious establishment can sometimes be less than helpful to those seeking Jesus.* Herod and the religious leaders did not genuinely receive the wise men. Rather, they treated them with suspicion and fear. Herod's true concern was not to worship the newborn king but to protect his status. We must ask God to increase our love for others so that our love becomes stronger than our fears and insecurities.

• *People need more than "facts."* They need partnership and direction on their journeys. The religious leaders of the day were able to interpret the Old Testament prophets properly, but they never left Jerusalem to travel with the wise men to Bethlehem to worship Christ. Followers of Jesus cannot remain inside the church, offering only words and interpretations to those on the outside. We are to walk alongside people where they are, at whatever stage of spiritual exploration they have reached.

## Resources

William Barclay, *Matthew*, The Daily Study Bible (Philadelphia: Westminster, 1975).

W. Hulitt Gloer, "Magi," *Mercer Dictionary of the Bible*, ed. Watson E. Mills (Macon GA: Mercer University Press, 1990).

Sherman E. Johnson, "Matthew" (exegesis), *The Interpreter's Bible*, vol. 7 (Nashville: Abingdon, 1979).

Ronnie McBrayer, *Leaving Religion, Following Jesus* (Macon GA: Smyth & Helwys, 2009).

# WHERE IS THE CHILD?

*Matthew 2:1-12*

## Looking for Wisdom

Every December, our family takes a walk to get a closer look at the nativity scene two blocks from our house. Mary always wears blue. Jesus, who looks about two years old, wears pajamas—not the normal translation for "swaddling clothes." Joseph and the only shepherd could pass for twins. Apparently, this shepherd is not good at his job; he tends only one sheep. An angel playing a harp leans against the flagpole. Santa Claus shimmies down a rope while four reindeer wait on the roof. Three turbaned wise men stand in a line, bearing gifts that resemble a jewelry box, a golden football, and a silver sausage. The visitors from the east look at least as out of place as Santa.

Matthew's version of the first Christmas has little in common with Luke's more popular account. Trying to put the two stories together is confusing. The shift is dramatic: exit Luke's shepherds, enter Matthew's magi; exit stable, enter palace; exit poverty, enter wealth; exit angels, enter dreams; exit Mary's lullaby, enter Rachel's crying. Both Matthew and Luke at least emphasize traveling. The story is about people making trips: from Nazareth to Bethlehem; from the fields to the manger; from Judea to Egypt. The best known, longest, and most unlikely journey is that of the magi from Persia to Palestine, a trip for which a GPS would not even try to give directions. What if wise women instead of wise men had gone to Bethlehem? They would have asked for directions, arrived on time, delivered the baby, and brought practical gifts.

This unreasonable trip had no reasonable beginning. What started them on their way? Matthew implies that the trip began with an unexplainable longing. Something unaccountable led the magi to follow a light without knowing where it would take them.

Matthew wants us to see beyond the familiar. We all long for God. We do not always recognize this desire for what it is, but we feel it. Our spirits hunger for meaning, our souls for hope, and our hearts for love.

Why do we read the Bible? Why do we study a passage like Matthew 2:1-12? We have mixed motives, but at least part of our reason is the faint hope that we will feel God's presence. We read the Bible, even without recognizing that we read in response to a longing. We are called forth like the magi, led by the light of a star. We feel the pull of God's love.

The longing is so deep and the voice so distant that even in the moments when we think we feel something, we do not often take even a single step forward. We find it less frightening to stay where we are than to move toward a light that we are not certain we saw. For every three far-seeing, truly wise persons, there are a hundred who will not see beyond their noses. Most of us are too practical to chase stars.

## The Wise Men in Jerusalem (Mt 2:1-8)

After Jesus was born in the village of Bethlehem, the band of scholars arrived in Jerusalem. Matthew calls them "magi," not "wise men" or "kings." The word "magi" is the root from which we get our word "magician." A magus was a sorcerer and scientist, an astrologer and astronomer, a physicist and physician, and a metaphysicist, too. Science and superstition were not yet separated, and the magi dabbled in all of it.

Something like magic may be the point—not magic in the sense of hocus pocus, but magic that opens the mind to the wonder of existence. One way of thinking about magic is understanding that there is more to life than we usually recognize.

The wise men come looking for wisdom, but we do not know much else about them, so we have created our own ideas. One early tradition is that there were twelve magi, but that crowded the crèche. Since the Bible lists three gifts for little Jesus, shaky evidence though it is, we went with three wise men. The carol

"We Three Kings" is fixed in our minds. Some have even provided names for the wise men—Gaspar, Melchior, and Balthasar—and identify them as representing different races.

With their star charts and whatever passed for telescopes fifteen hundred years before their invention, the magi came to the peculiar conclusion that a new king was born in Israel. Matthew found it significant that the wise men were Gentiles in the heartland of Judaism.

Six hundred years earlier, Isaiah predicted the pilgrimage of rich kings to Jerusalem to worship God, bringing gifts of gold and frankincense. Scholars believe Isaiah 60 influenced Matthew's telling of the story.

One legend is that the journey took thirty days. A trip like that was uncommon—a long distance, short-lived night fires, sore-footed camels, unfriendly towns, the danger of bandits, the uncertainty of what lay behind the next sand dune. An unexplainable longing sent the stargazers on this unreasonable trip.

As our passage describes, the magi finally arrive in Jerusalem and ask, "Where can we find the newborn king of the Jews? We saw a star that signaled his birth. We've come to worship him."

The news terrified Herod—and most of Jerusalem as well. Herod the Great ruled from about 37–4 BC. (The New Testament also mentions three of his sons, a grandson, and a great-grandson.) The people were afraid because they knew how unbalanced King Herod could be. Herod executed some members of his own family. Anyone worthy of worship threatened his position. Herod was a fake king of the Jews, put in power by the Romans. He constantly feared for his job, or at least that his remaining sons would not inherit his throne.

Herod called together the "chief priests and scribes," the leaders of the religious establishment, and asked them where the Messiah was to be born. Technically, only one chief priest served at a time. The scribes were the Old Testament scholars.

They told him, "Bethlehem in the territory of Judah. The prophet Micah wrote it plainly." Second Samuel 5:2 may also figure into their conclusion. John 7:42 makes reference to the belief that the Messiah will come from Bethlehem. The scribes are smart enough to remember Micah 5:2, but not wise enough to look for the child themselves.

Herod arranged a meeting with the magi. He pretended to be as devout as they were and got them to tell him exactly when the starry birth announcement appeared. The deceitful Herod suggested they conduct a thorough search and tried to hoodwink the magi into coming back to tell him the child's location so that he could pay the child a visit, too.

## The Wise Men in Bethlehem (Mt 2:9-12)

When the magi set off, the star appeared again and led them to the child. They could hardly contain themselves. They entered the house and threw the most famous baby shower ever. Unlike Luke, Matthew gives no hint that Joseph and Mary are merely stopping in Bethlehem for the census. Matthew seems to imply that Bethlehem was their home (see 2:22-23). Surely Mary and Joseph were confused as the magi celebrated finding their way to the long-awaited hope.

The strangers from the east opened their treasure chest, offering gifts of gold, frankincense, and myrrh—a precious metal and costly aromatic gum resins from shrubs found in tropical countries. The magi's visit lasts all of one verse. Matthew does not give us details. We are not told if they stayed for dinner, what they thought, what they felt, or if Mary traded the myrrh for diapers. What did the magi see when they looked into the face of the newborn child?

The mysterious travelers were out of place in Bethlehem. Imagine a group of Saudi Arabian sultans stopping at a Dairy Queen in the Delta of Mississippi. The magi were urban in a rural setting, affluent in the midst of poverty, and cultured and cosmopolitan in an uneducated town, but wisdom led them there.

A dream warned them not to report back to Herod. They found another route, left the territory without being seen, and returned to their own country. This is the last we see or hear of the wise men.

## Following the Star

The magi make several contributions to Matthew's Gospel. First, they are an early indication of the universal character of the gospel. Jesus later calls his followers to make disciples of "all nations" (Mt 28:19). At the same time, the wise men introduce Herod and his murderous hostility to Christ. This antagonism is evident in the Jerusalem authorities all the way to the crucifixion. Third, the wise men and their gifts teach us a lesson in authentic worship. Finally, the wise men are an example of how genuine wisdom leads to Christ.

Matthew may tell this story out of frustration that the majority of Jews dismissed Jesus and persecuted his followers. Gentiles rather than Jews followed the star. The magi represent the wisdom that recognizes life as a journey in search of the one who calls us beyond ourselves, one before whom we should kneel and to whom we should offer the best of our gifts. What makes one truly wise is understanding the hope that is in this child.

We should be open to wisdom wherever we find it. Too many mistakenly limit their search to what they can see and measure. Only the facts are worthy of attention for such people. They perceive the intellectual as opposing the spiritual. Many quickly dismiss faith, eternal life, and anything that smacks of the sacred.

Atheists argue that science has made religion unnecessary, but their arguments are not convincing. The fact that nature obeys precise mathematical laws, the fact that life and mind have emerged from inanimate matter, and the fact that the universe exists at all are best explained by God beyond what we can see and measure.

It seems that the skeptics try to convince themselves that life can have meaning without God, but it is not true. Without God, life lacks spirit or heart. To choose disbelief and skepticism is to miss the truths of faith and spirituality. Cynicism leads to a dull, routine, and ultimately despairing view of life.

The truly wise leave their minds open to possibilities farther out and deeper within. We should imagine more than we can explain, confess that we need to believe, and admit our sense of the sacred. We should look for the wisdom of the Spirit, the wisdom of Christ.

In most of the Gospel stories, Jesus goes looking for people, intrudes into their lives, or moves into their villages and homes. In Matthew's story of the magi, they come looking for Jesus. No one travels farther to see him than they do.

The wise men followed even though it seemed foolish. They wanted to see Jesus more than they wanted to keep their treasures, more than they wanted to play it safe, and more than they feared the difficulties of the journey.

The Christian faith is not merely a set of beliefs, but a willingness to travel and pursue God's gentle light. Christianity is more than a place to stand; it is a direction in which to move. People who play their faith safely soon have no faith to play.

Is the one who follows the star the fool, or is it the many who remain in the darkness? Are we courageous enough to seek God's wisdom? Are we willing to relinquish our sense of control and go where Jesus leads us? Can we rise to a new sense of adventure, forsake our cozy boundaries, and seek Christ?

God calls us to be open to the wisdom that will help us be more than we are. The baby that the magi found was not the end of the journey; he was the beginning. We do not merely *believe* in Jesus. We *follow* Jesus. Christ takes us places where we would never go without his leading. We have a desert to travel, a star to discover, and life to find.

# Notes

# Notes

# A VOICE WAS HEARD IN RAMAH

*Matthew 2:13-23*

## Central Question

What can Christmas say about the problem of human suffering?

## Scripture

**Matthew 2:13-23** Now after they had left, an angel of the Lord appeared to Joseph in a dream and said, "Get up, take the child and his mother, and flee to Egypt, and remain there until I tell you; for Herod is about to search for the child, to destroy him." 14 Then Joseph got up, took the child and his mother by night, and went to Egypt, 15 and remained there until the death of Herod. This was to fulfill what had been spoken by the Lord through the prophet, "Out of Egypt I have called my son." 16 When Herod saw that he had been tricked by the wise men, he was infuriated, and he sent and killed all the children in and around Bethlehem who were two years old or under, according to the time that he had learned from the wise men. 17 Then was fulfilled what had been spoken through the prophet Jeremiah: 18 "A voice was heard in Ramah, wailing and loud lamentation, Rachel weeping for her children; she refused to be consoled, because they are no more." 19 When Herod died, an angel of the Lord suddenly appeared in a dream to Joseph in Egypt and said, 20 "Get up, take the child and his mother, and go to the land of Israel, for those who were seeking the child's life are dead." 21 Then Joseph got up, took the child and his mother, and went to the land of Israel. 22 But when he heard that Archelaus was ruling over Judea in place of his father Herod, he was afraid to go there. And after being warned in a dream, he went away to the district of Galilee. 23 There he made his home in a town called Nazareth, so that what had been spoken through the prophets might be fulfilled, "He will be called a Nazorean."

## Reflecting

William Barclay recalls the following legend:

> When Joseph and Mary and Jesus were on their way to Egypt, the story runs, as the evening came they were weary, and they sought refuge in a cave. It was very cold, so cold that the ground was white with frost. A little spider saw the little baby Jesus, and he wished so much that he could do something to keep Him warm in the cold night. He decided to do the only thing he could and spin his web across the entrance of the cave, to make, as it were, a curtain there.
>
> Along the path came a detachment of Herod's soldiers, seeking for children to kill to carry out Herod's bloodthirsty order. When they came to the cave they were about to burst in to search it, but their captain noticed the spider's web, covered with the white frost and stretched right across the entrance to the cave.
>
> "Look," he said, "at the spider's web there. It is quite unbroken and there cannot possibly be anyone in the cave, for anyone entering would certainly have torn the web."
>
> So the soldiers passed on, and left the holy family in peace, because a little spider had spun his web across the entrance to the cave. And that, so they say, is why to this day we put tinsel on our Christmas trees, for the glittering tinsel streamers stand for the spider's web, white with frost stretched across the entrance of the cave on the way to Egypt. (35)

While this story is only a myth, it is true that Jesus and his parents escaped the murderous plot of Herod into Egypt. Many other children and families did not. How could God allow such a horrendous event to take place? How does Christmas speak to such injustice?

## Studying

The story of the visiting magi typically ends with the exchange of their precious gifts at the feet of Jesus and their journey back home as changed men (Mt 2:1-12). But their search for Messiah set off a chain of events in the little town of Bethlehem that was the opposite of "peace on earth." It was ugly, violent, unjust, and all too familiar in the hazardous world in which we live.

When King Herod realized that the magi were not returning to Jerusalem to disclose the location of the promised Messiah, he initiated a desperate plan to eliminate competitors for his throne. He ordered the murder of all male children age two and younger in the vicinity of Bethlehem (v. 16).

The Bethlehem infanticide is not recorded in any other historical documents, but this should come as no surprise. While tragic, this event was a minor occurrence in a backwater village of Herod's kingdom. Bethlehem was a small town, and this act of vengeance involved only a few families and maybe only a dozen or so children. In light of Herod's greater crimes, secular historians considered this event of little importance.

> In a sense [Christianity] creates, rather than solves, the problem of pain, for pain would be no problem unless side by side with our daily experience of this painful world, we had received what we think a good assurance that ultimate reality is righteousness and loving.
> —C. S. Lewis

Still, to say that only a few children died in an insignificant village does not make this act less horrible. In some ways, it actually sharpens the injustice. Why murder these few children? What possible threat could a few babies and toddlers pose to an old, dying king? How could a society tolerate such overt wrongdoing? Where was God as Herod carried out this destruction of innocent life?

In this story, Jesus does not die for the salvation of others; he escapes. After a dream warns Joseph of the coming danger, he flees to Egypt in the night with Mary and

> Jesus is a new Moses, and Herod is another Pharaoh.... The "slaughter of the innocents" evokes Ex 1. NT 5

Jesus (v. 13). Jesus, Joseph, and Mary remained there until the threat against Jesus' life subsided. In verse 15, Matthew quotes

the prophet Hosea: "Out of Egypt I called my son" (Hos 11:1). This verse refers to the exodus, when Moses led the nation of Israel out of Egypt to the promised land. With these words, Matthew lends credibility to the ministry and identity of the Messiah. Jesus would not remain in Egypt, but would come out like the nation of Israel and reenter the Jewish homeland (vv. 19-20).

In many ways, Jesus' life and ministry recreated Israel's history. He fled to Egypt for safety but ultimately returned, retracing the steps of the exodus. He was baptized and crossed over the Jordan as his forbearers once crossed the Red Sea. He was in the desert for forty days and forty nights; the children of Israel spent forty years in the desert. By identifying with his people in this way, he also identified with their suffering. He entered the injustice of the world, and it eventually crushed him. However, he overcame the injustice and redeemed the world.

Even Jesus' return to the city of Nazareth was a subtle sign of God's entering the suffering of the world. Nazareth had a poor reputation. Even one of the first disciples initially balked at following Jesus because of his hometown, asking sarcastically, "Can anything good come out of Nazareth" (Jn 1:44-46)?

> If souls can suffer alongside, and I hardly know it, because the spirit of discernment is not in me, then I know nothing of Calvary love.
> —Amy Carmichael

Nazareth had its own brand and depth of pain. In the years of Jesus' childhood, there were no fewer than three major messianic movements in Galilee. Three legions of Roman soldiers poured into the region to squash these rebellions. The resulting slaughter was cataclysmic. Cities were burned to the ground, people were put in chains, and the Romans crucified 2,000 men and women (Crossan, 199).

Where was God in the midst of this? God was in the person of Jesus, suffering with those under the heavy hand of injustice. Jesus did not avoid suffering and rarely explained it. But he did embrace it and bring redemption from it. God is in all things, joining his children in their sufferings.

The accusation that God is absent from the creation cannot stand. God is in the world, celebrating our victories, enduring our hardships, and bearing our hurts. God may not always rescue us, but God always identifies with us and will never abandon us. We are not alone.

## Understanding

On February 15, 1947, Glenn Chambers boarded a plan bound for Quito, Ecuador. He was beginning his career as a missionary to the native tribes there. He never arrived; his plane crashed in the mountains of South America.

Moments before Glenn left the Miami airport, he jotted a note to his mother. All he found to write on was a piece of advertising paper. He scribbled his message on the back of the advertisement. By accident or providence, Chambers had picked up an advertisement with a single word on the front. In bold black letters, all caps, was the question, *WHY?*

When Chambers's mother read the note after her son's death, the first word she saw was not part of Glenn's hurried message. Like a haunting voice from the grave, the first thing she saw was the question, *WHY?*

"Why?" We have all asked this question. Why do good people suffer? Why are loved ones struck with cancer? Why do children die before they have the opportunity to reach adulthood? Why do marriages fail? Why does God seem so far away? Why is life so unfair?

Millions have suffered angst and disillusionment in the face of unfair circumstances. In the pain of life, when it all comes crashing in, people often feel abandoned and forsaken by God. But God has abandoned no one. Rather than standing at a distance, God has entered this world of pain and suffered its worst injustices. In the person of Jesus, God came as the best man ever to live and took on the very worst of life.

The quotation "He will be called a Nazorean" is not found anywhere in the Old Testament. Since netzer is the Hebrew word for "branch," the saying may be a word play on the promise of a righteous branch from the royal line of David (Isa 11:1; Jer 33:15).

Advent reveals a God who does not ignore or intellectualize the problem when he hears the cry, "I feel alone" or "This is not fair." Rather, God has chosen to identify with this feeling, for God has been there himself (McBrayer, 36).

## What About Me?

• *Faith in God does not insulate us from tragedy or injustice.* Following Christ or having faith in God does not guarantee a trouble-free life. Nor will having "more faith" lead to less difficulty in this unfair world. Faith cannot protect a believer from suffering unfairness, but it can empower the believer to bear injustice with patience and hope.

• *There is sometimes no definitive explanation for suffering in the world.* Supposedly "biblical" explanations that attempt to account for the suffering in the world are shallow at best and disingenuous at worst. Many tragedies—corporate and personal—are beyond human understanding. We must wait patiently for resolution, and even then the answer to the question "why" may not materialize in this lifetime.

• *God's silence in the face of suffering does not mean God is unaware, unconcerned, or uninvolved.* God has entered the world in the person of Jesus Christ. Jesus has suffered in all ways, even as humanity suffers. Being subjected to the frailties and injustices of the world has enabled Christ to sympathize with our weaknesses and hardships.

• *People of faith don't have to explain evil.* Rather, they are called to enter with empathy the lives of those who have been harmed. To practice the presence of Christ is to love and interact with those who have experienced the worst the world offers. Those who have suffered deeply often do not need explanations as much as they need compassion.

• *Christmas is a symbol of God's coming kingdom when all suffering, injustice, and tragedy will be defeated.* At Christmas, Christians celebrate the arrival of Christ into the world, but also look forward to his final coming and consummation of the kingdom of God when all things will be made new.

## Resources

William Barclay, *The Gospel of Matthew*, The Daily Study Bible Series (Philadelphia: Westminster, 1975).

John Dominic Crossan, *The Historical Jesus: The Life of a Mediterranean Jewish Peasant* (New York: HarperColllins, 1991).

Ronnie McBrayer, *Keeping the Faith: Passages, Proverbs, Parables* (Freeport FL: Leaving Salem Projects, 2008).

# A VOICE WAS HEARD
# IN RAMAH

### *Matthew 2:13-23*

## Almost a Hallmark Card

Over twenty Christmases ago, I was the new pastor of Central
Baptist Church in Paoli, Indiana. I decided to have a Christmas
Eve candlelight Communion service—the first ever at the church.
I wanted everything to be perfect, and it almost was. Snow fell
that afternoon. A junior in high school played "What Child Is
This" on the flute. Three generations—a grandmother, her
daughter, and granddaughter—lit the Advent candles. We sang
the carols "O Come All Ye Faithful," "Away in a Manger," and
"O Little Town of Bethlehem." We read the story—Mary, Joseph,
and the baby. I remember thinking, "This is a Hallmark card of a
worship service. This is as picture perfect a Christmas moment as
any church has ever known."

Then Danny's beeper went off. Danny was a member of the
volunteer fire department. When his beeper sounded, as it often
did—and it was ten times as likely to go off in church as
anywhere else—Danny ran out of the sanctuary. We had gotten
used to it, but it was still disconcerting. Then we started singing
"Silent Night." Just as we got to "Wondrous Star, lend thy light"
Danny ran back in to say that Bob's mother's house was on fire.
Bob, his wife, Linda, and their daughter, Melody, ran out after
Danny. Then Danny's wife got up and left.

Everyone there had to choose between listening to the sermon
or slipping out one by one and going to a really big fire. By the
time I got Mary and Joseph to Bethlehem, the crowd—and I use
that term loosely—was made up of those waiting for a ride home
and those sleeping. That is not how Christmas Eve candlelight
Communion services are supposed to turn out. Tragedies should

wait until January because they do not fit our ideas about Christmas.

## Keeping Herod in Christmas

That is why King Herod does not fit the Christmas story. The horrifying sequence of events in Matthew's Gospel feels out of place. The most difficult part to cast in the Christmas pageant is King Herod. Wal-Mart sells a variety of plastic nativity scenes for the yard, but there are no glow-in-the-dark King Herods. No Christmas card has this verse from Matthew on the front—"a voice was heard in Ramah, wailing and loud lamentation" (Mt 2:18). This part may not seem to fit, but we need to hear it. We must hear the whole story, or we get the story wrong.

We tend to think of Christmas as sweetness and light, good tidings and great joy. Our decorations are pretty: Mary in bright blue ceramics; glass angels on the tree; wooden mangers that look like baby beds. Most Christmas decorations are not from Matthew's Gospel, but from Luke's. Luke has the manger, Mary, shepherds, and the sky filled with angels. Matthew has Joseph and Mary in a house, and Herod trying to kill Jesus. Most Christmas music is from Luke. Luke has lullabies. Matthew has the screams of mothers. Luke is rated G. Matthew is rated R for violence.

We leave King Herod out of the Christmas story because we think we are supposed to keep the hardships of the real world away from Christmas. But if tragedy and Christmas do not go together, then why do we have this part of the story?

Matthew says Christmas came in the days of King Herod (2:1). King Herod is like Joseph Stalin. He executed his favorite wife, his brother-in-law, and three of his sons because he thought they wanted his crown. The Roman Emperor Augustus used a play on words when he said that it was better to be Herod's pig (*hys*) than Herod's son (*hyios*).

King Herod was understandably afraid that when he died the Jewish people would celebrate. He left an order (which was not followed) that on the day of his death, the oldest child in each Israelite home would be put to death. When Herod was troubled, all Jerusalem was troubled with him (2:3). When the wise men told him about the new king, Herod was troubled. If they were truly wise, they should have been suspicious when Herod asked for later news of the baby so he could come and pay his respects to the new king. After they found the baby, the magi had a dream telling them they should not go back to Herod's palace.

## Fleeing from Bethlehem to Egypt (Mt 2:13-15)

After the wise men left, Joseph also had a dream warning him of Herod's plans. We usually imagine angels speaking in soft, reassuring tones. This angel must have shouted: "Wake up! Hurry! Run!"

They fled to Egypt. They were far from home, but the baby was safe.

Egypt was a Roman province outside Herod's authority. There was a large Jewish colony in Egypt—nearly a million people according to Philo of Alexandria. By 150 BC, Egyptian Jews had their own temple at Leontopolis.

Sources outside Matthew refer to Jesus' time in Egypt. The early church father Origen addressed a tradition that Jesus worked in Egypt as a laborer, learned magic there, and returned to Judea claiming to be a god. Perhaps he responded to Matthew's account, but if the rumors were independent, then Matthew may have attempted to counteract an unwanted tradition by showing that Jesus was only a small child while in Egypt, not a grown man learning magic, and that he was taken there for protection from Herod and brought back under divine guidance.

Matthew said this Egyptian exile fulfilled what the prophet had preached years earlier. Hosea 11:1 referred to Israel as God's "son" whom God called out of Egypt in the time of Moses. Matthew applies this to Jesus, God's Son in whom a new people were to be constituted.

Matthew suggests parallels between Jesus and Moses. Just as Moses fled Egypt to escape the pharaoh and returned when the pharaoh was dead, so Jesus was hurried away to escape Herod and returned after Herod's death. Just as God called Israel out of Egypt, so Jesus is called out of Egypt to save his people.

This story includes themes that recur throughout Matthew: Jesus rejected at home, God's guidance at every point, the foreshadowing of Jesus' suffering, and the fulfillment of Old Testament expectations.

## Herod Kills Infants in Bethlehem (Mt 2:16-18)

Joseph's dream caused Herod's plot to fail, but not everyone was as safe as Jesus. Herod's order that all male children under two be killed implies that Jesus was older than one or that Herod made the limits wider than necessary, not caring how many died.

Herod probably did not believe that God sent a Messiah to Israel, but he did worry that a popular figure might threaten his position. The massacre of babies is too awful to imagine. Mothers cried in anguish as Herod's soldiers cut their children's throats.

Matthew cannot find words terrifying enough to describe the horror, so he borrows them from the prophet (Jer 31:15): "weeping and great mourning, Rachel weeping for her children; she refuses to be consoled, because they are no more."

Rachel, according to tradition, was buried between Jerusalem and Bethlehem. Jeremiah referred to Rachel's weeping over the Ephraimites going into Babylonian exile. Matthew applies the verse to the sorrow at Bethlehem, near where Rachel was buried.

## Returning from Egypt to Nazareth (Mt 2:19-23)

Since Herod died in 4 BC, the birth of Jesus is usually dated around 6 BC. Herod's will designated his son Archelaus to be king of Judea, Samaria, and Idumea. Another son, Antipas, became tetrarch of Galilee and Perea. Augustus denied Archelaus the title of "king," instead holding it out as a reward for effective government. Augustus gave him the title "ethnarch" and ended up banishing Archelaus in AD 6.

When Herod died, God's angel appeared in a dream to Joseph in Egypt: "Take the child and his mother and go back to Israel. Those out to murder the child are dead" (2:20).

When Joseph heard that Archelaus had succeeded his father as ruler in Judea, he was afraid to go there. Again, a dream directed him elsewhere—this time to the hills of Galilee.

Matthew has no reticence about dreams. An angel told Joseph that God was the father of Mary's child, the wise men were warned in a dream not to go back to Herod, an angel in a dream sent Joseph and his family to Egypt, a dream told Joseph it was time to go back to Israel, and a dream sent Joseph to Galilee. Matthew's purpose is to show that both the flight into Egypt and the return to Nazareth fulfilled Scripture.

## The Hard Side of Christmas

We usually skip the detail of the Holy Innocents when we tell the Christmas story. The senseless murder of babies is out of place amid the sentimentality that fills the season. The story seems theologically backward. Jesus is safe while innocent children die.

The first Christmas included soldiers with swords in the streets while mothers clutched their babies, hiding in the closet, trying not to breathe too loudly, and begging their infants not to cry. The first Christmas was not sweetness and light for these mothers and fathers. There are not many questions more impossible to answer than, "Why couldn't the angel have warned them, too?" Even the birth of the new King did not stop suffering.

This difficult story challenges believers to rise above sentimentality and address the hardest issues raised by Christmas. It is not surprising that we skip this part of the story. It is easy to understand why no carol in our hymnals addresses the slaughter of the innocents. Perhaps one should, because we need to understand that suffering and Christmas do in fact belong together. Christmas is God's response to our sorrows.

Christmas is not good news of a great joy that will make everything easy. Joseph was the father of a son who was not quite his. How did he feel when strangers said, "He must look like his mother"? Mary was not old enough to be married under the best of circumstances. Now she was far from home with a newborn to care for. Christmas is not about a king born to luxury, but an infant born to peasants in a rundown section of an obscure Roman province, out behind a cheap motel among cattle and sheep, laid in a feed trough in moldy hay. God came into the noise and storms, wind and wailing, dying children, raging soldiers and devastated parents.

## Christmas and Suffering

During my second Christmas season as pastor of Central Baptist Church in Paoli, Indiana, I got a phone call from the county hospital on December 23. The night before, an unwed teenager gave birth to a stillborn baby. The social worker wanted me to lead a graveside service the next morning. She explained that they would normally have the service a day later or at least in the afternoon, but she "didn't want the girl to associate this experience with Christmas." The teenager had visited our church a few times several months earlier. She was fifteen and had been raped by her grandfather.

Christmas Eve was miserable. The snow had been on the ground for more than a week. Rain had turned it into frozen, muddy slush. The temperature was in the twenties. It was dark and threatening to rain again. The young girl's older sister brought her straight from the hospital. Their parents did not come. They blamed her for what had happened. Six of us stood there at the funeral home: the girl, her sister, the funeral director, two women from our church, and me. I knew what I had been told: "We don't want her to associate this experience with Christmas," but I kept thinking about the story that Matthew tells. Christmas is about mothers crying because their children have died: "wailing and loud lamentation, weeping and great mourning,...refusing to be consoled, because they are no more." If we have to stand at a graveside on Christmas Eve, we need to remember the hope that comes with Christmas.

The part of this story that we are used to leaving out—the sadness, suffering, and death—is most important. It is the hard part that explains why this Child is a holy Child.

# Notes

# Notes